MW01030781

THE
INVISIBLE
CORSET

THE

BREAK FREE FROM BEAUTY

INVISIBLE

CULTURE AND EMBRACE

CORSET

YOUR RADIANT SELF

LAUREN GEERTSEN

sounds true
BOULDER, COLORADO

Sounds True
Boulder, CO 80306

Published 2021

Book design by Maureen Forys, Happenstance Type-O-Rama

Printed in Canada

Library of Congress Cataloging-in-Publication Data
Names: Geertsen, Lauren, author.
Title: The invisible corset : break free from beauty culture and embrace
    your radiant self / Lauren Geertsen.
Description: Boulder, CO : Sounds True, 2021. | Includes bibliographical
    references.
Identifiers: LCCN 2020016773 (print) | LCCN 2020016774 (ebook) | ISBN
    9781683646181 (hardcover) | ISBN 9781683646198 (ebook)
Subjects: LCSH: Self-acceptance in women. | Self-esteem in women. | Body
    image in women.
Classification: LCC BF575.S37 G44 2021 (print) | LCC BF575.S37 (ebook) |
    DDC 306.4/613--dc23
LC record available at https://lccn.loc.gov/2020016773
LC ebook record available at https://lccn.loc.gov/2020016774

For the daughters.

DISCLAIMER

CONTENTS

May you realize your body is a faithful and beautiful friend of your soul.

—JOHN O'DONOHUE

PROLOGUE

The divorce rate between women and our bodies is sky-high.

We're told our worth is our beauty, and our glory is youth, and we're told this so often we swallow it as truth.

Beauty culture clamors, "Change yourself, rearrange yourself, shrink, shape, and buy!" We slather our skin with promises, but our bodies never seem to comply.

"I'm choosing this," we say, "because I prefer to look this way." But what about that small inner voice that says, "I sort of like it . . . but partly, I don't feel like I have a choice."

We're afraid of our weight, our size, our face, our skin. We learn to see our bodies' uniqueness as our special brand of sin.

The industry of patriarchy has told us beauty is pain, and we need beauty to win this survival game. We concede, and so internalize our oppression, holding our bonds in place with our own perceptions.

We believe beauty is our currency, a required vocation, so we spend more on beauty than we do on our education. It's a worthwhile investment, or so we believe, as if "thin and pretty" is required praise we must achieve.

Eventually, we find our bodies too poorly equipped for a lasting relationship. "My body failed me," we cry. So day after day, we pack our bags and prepare to give our bodies a final good-bye.

Some women spit sparks of rage and scream, "I can't do this anymore!" as we slam the door. And yet others say, with eyes full of longing as we walk away, "Body, why did you make it impossible for me to love you?"

When women decide our bodies have failed us, we begin our search for a new home. We knock on the doors of money, lovers, friends, children, careers, food and drugs, products and prestige. We ask, of everyone and everything else, the question weighing down our soul:

"Will you love me enough so that I can feel whole?"

We are going out of our minds, looking for the love we left behind.

We've spent years battling the natural circumstances of our bodies. But how can we find our way back to ourselves when we are trying to escape ourselves?

We must look in the mirror and see ourselves clearly. Shall we give up the fight? Shall we give ourselves over to the ocean of our untamed light?

The truth of our bodies stands before us, hidden in plain sight.

Remember, our beauty is not something to earn.

It's time to unlace the corset and let our true beauty return.

INTRODUCTION

As a little girl, I wanted to do fabulous and creative things with my hands, voice, and body. I wanted to be a professional dog sitter, a singer, an athlete, a dancer, an architect, a businesswoman, a writer. I spent school recess either tearing across the playfield after a soccer ball or madly scribbling a story in a lined notebook. On early weekend mornings, before the family woke up, I'd sketch out palatial floor plans for my dream bedroom. I saved Halloween candy, lined it up on my bookshelf, and in July, opened a candy store for my friends.

Being myself was all I knew how to be, and I liked being myself. Then, gradually but also quite suddenly, things changed. At the cusp of puberty, I put aside what I wanted *to do* and instead wanted *to be* beautiful. I remember examining the products in my mom's bathroom at that time. There was the hair smoother, the self-tanner, the lip plumper, the skin primer, the cellulite cream. I did the logic backward: this meant her hair was too frizzy, complexion too pale, lips too thin, skin too textured.

After careful consideration, the implications hit me: My hair was hers, the same color and curl. My skin was hers, the same shade of porcelain. My lips and complexion, like hers, were worthy of rejection. At the brink of puberty, I realized the fate of being in the wrong body was coming at me like a freight train. I, too, needed to line up products like soldiers on the bathroom counter and battle my body.

I also needed beauty the same way I needed academic accolades. Here was the yardstick of enoughness: I just had to make my hair gleam, and chisel my abs like the women in magazines. I didn't question that yardstick but rather lunged for it. It seemingly offered me the opportunity to feel okay about myself in a world that told me, "You're not measuring up." Maybe I wasn't born with it, just like I wasn't born getting straight As, but with enough time, money, and discipline, I could climb the ladder of adequacy.

So I poured my time and babysitting money into concealing, shaping, toning, straightening, smoothing, and shrinking myself. The more I tried to change my body, however, the more I hated it. And the more I hated my body, the more I disliked being me.

Body hatred stems from the belief that our appearance makes us incapable or unworthy of our destiny, and it manifests in the attempt to change our appearance instead of a toxic societal system. Body hatred silences the women's souls. Like a rope, it is around the waist of every newborn girl and is yanked tightly when she gets big and bold enough to be a force of curiosity, sensuality, and self-expression in the world. When it comes to our pursuit of beauty, it's not the intention that counts but the result. We intend to find confidence, happiness, and worthiness. The results, however, are exhaustion, frustration, and despair that we pass down from generation to generation.

As the years passed, I started to remember what it felt like to *want my own life*. I daydreamed about plunging into a pool without worrying about my makeup or my thighs. I yearned to eat a luxurious lunch without calculating my caloric intake. I ached to enjoy a vacation without panicking over a missed workout. I longed to relax under the gaze of a lover without feeling the need to apologize for my bloated stomach. I felt soul hungry, haunted by the echoes of untasted opportunities.

Most of all, I wanted to let myself *out*: to bask and feast and roam in this beautiful world. Yet a rigid, intangible pressure weighed upon me, making me feel trapped by body inadequacies. I was ravenous for life, but the invisible corset held me in place.

In order to like myself and my life again, I needed to learn how to stop hating my body. I would have to untie the thousands of years of restrictive beliefs that were bound around my psyche.

This book is the treasure map I made as I traveled the path from body shame to body connection and soul-expanding confidence. As a Body Connection Coach, I guide my clients on the same journey. This book provides the steps and insight you'll need to like your body, and yourself, again. Even if you've hated your body for decades, feel disillusioned with prior attempts at body positivity, or believe that self-acceptance is a lost cause, this book will show you how to find body liberation.

THIS IS A RELATIONSHIP GUIDE— NOT A CONTROL MANUAL

Perhaps reading this book isn't the first attempt you've made at improving your relationship with your body. If your journey is like mine, you've tried to stop hating your body for years by controlling her better. You've tried to dominate, twist, silence, and exhaust her into complying with what you think will make you happy. Maybe you've compared her to other bodies, and tried to force her into someone she isn't. But if controlling your body worked, then:

- dieting would be effective, making you both thin and ecstatically happy;

- an intricate skincare routine would alleviate your anxiety;

- that "holy grail" of mascara or concealer would make you 100 percent confident—even when you wash it off;

- Botox and anti-aging creams would put to rest any fears of your body changing with time.

Ironically, the more we try to control our bodies, the more out of control we feel in our lives. No matter how hard we try to stop them, our bodies change or refuse to change. Wrinkles appear, bellies soften, gray hairs sprout, the "baby weight" remains. We feel hardened, depleted, and burned-out from fighting our bodies. Anxiety arises, since it is a symptom of trying to control what one cannot control. Eventually, we lose touch with the joy of having a body.

Our bodies hold a force of nature greater and more powerful than we are, and if we fight our bodies, we lock ourselves in a losing battle. Control isn't the solution; it's the problem. Body control keeps us disconnected from our bodies, in a state of perpetual body insecurity rather than peace. Perhaps you've experienced this in your relationships. When someone is controlling you through their physical, emotional, or financial power, you don't feel connected to them. Instead, you feel resentful and bitter and want to get away from them. When control is the glue holding a relationship together, ease and safety eludes you, and you can't rest in the arms of trust.

It's time to try differently, not harder, and this book teaches you different. Unlike so many diet and wellness books, this is not a control manual, it's a relationship guide. You'll learn to connect to your body through love and trust so you no longer need to control her.

Throughout this book, I share journaling and mindset-changing exercises. This is the work of cutting your invisible corset strings. I suggest getting a fresh journal or notebook to do these exercises.

WHO AM I?

I'm Lauren Geertsen, and I work with clients around the world to heal their relationships with food and overcome body anxiety. I also created a health website, Empowered Sustenance, that's reached over forty million readers. I began the website to share my journey of healing my ulcerative colitis, an autoimmune disease that my doctors called "incurable." When all available medications failed me, and I was nearly bedridden due to my worsening disease, I turned to a nutrition protocol and holistic lifestyle changes that eliminated all my signs of disease and freed me from medication.

Taking this route took courage, determination, and self-trust. Ten years ago, the diet and therapies I used were considered unproven and unscientific. When it came to removing my own invisible corset, I took the same approach. I set out to heal the body insecurity that many others consider a life sentence. This required radical perspective changes and similarly unconventional approaches. Then, I analyzed my process and put it into the actionable steps in this book so you, too, can take off your invisible corset.

In part 1 of this book, I outline the five beliefs that make up the invisible corset strings: fear, domination, disconnection, mechanization, and coercion. In part 2, I equip you with specific practices that act as the scissors to cut those strings.

Do I Have It Easier?

I am a white woman and my body is small enough to fit comfortably in airplane seats. In my late twenties, I've sprouted only a few gray hairs, and my face looks youthful. With makeup, hair products, and good lighting, I resemble the "default white woman" you see in advertisements and media. Some of you may think, "Oh great, here's another woman talking about how hard it is to exist in her thin, Caucasian body." Or you might think, "If only I had her body, I'd be happy." And yet others might be thinking, "That describes me, and I've been miserable in my body for years."

Yes, I *have* had it easier in my body. I've likely never experienced discrimination because of my appearance, unlike those who exist in black, brown, fat, trans, disabled, or aged bodies. In fact, my appearance may have granted me unearned benefits. Data shows that I'm more likely to be seen as skilled and disciplined in work environments due to my body size, and that, since childhood, my conventional appearance meant teachers and peers were predisposed to think well of my personality. With that said, I am also qualified to tell you that being somewhat close to the beauty standard does not, in fact, make you happy. Body hatred, ultimately, is not about what we look like. It's about the belief that our bodies make us less worthy and lovable as human beings.

WHO IS THIS BOOK FOR?

In the early 1960s, culture was invested in women being happy housewives—think Mrs. Cleaver in *Leave It to Beaver*. Media and advertising circulated the message, "If you stay home to raise kids, keep your kitchen spotless, and cook three meals a day for your family, you will feel fulfillment and find inner peace." Women tried to conform to this standard, becoming housewives at an early age instead of pursuing higher education or work outside the home.

In her landmark book *The Feminine Mystique*, Betty Friedan validated the sense of existential emptiness so many housewives felt at the time. She made the invisible visible, calling it "the problem with no name." Finally, women could put words to the truth they felt: "I am spending all my energy being the perfect housewife, but I am anxious, bored, and soul-starved. Even the things that are supposed to make me happy, like a new vacuum cleaner or blender, aren't making me happy." Friedan gave women permission to feel the truth their bodies had been speaking all along, a truth that said, "My purpose in life extends beyond keeping a tidy home and preparing the perfect apple pie. I must use myself more fully and express my creativity and intellect, or I will go batshit crazy."

Women today find themselves in a similar trap. Whether we're students, young professionals, full-time moms or grandmothers, we feel anxious and constrained by body concerns 24/7. We're told we should just love our bodies and accept our flaws, but willpower alone can't undo the generations of brainwashing intended to repress women's confidence and power. Women know our purpose in life extends further than counting calories, losing pounds, and fighting wrinkles, but we're confined by the invisible corset.

In this book, I explain how beauty culture is an oppressive social system and an extension of patriarchy. At its roots, patriarchy arose from the desire to dominate and control women's biological functions—specifically our sexuality and ability to have babies. Societies that still reflect patriarchal values prohibit or limit women's sovereignty over our bodies, our sexuality, our labor, and our finances. This used to be accomplished through physical force. Now, as this book explains, it's done through more insidious and invisible means. Whereas society once limited women's freedom by saying, "Your place is in the home," it now restricts women with the message, "Your place is in a beautiful body." I wrote this book to help women of all ages to tune in to our bodies' truth so we can break the seams of the corset sewn together with fragile lies.

IS IT A BEAUTIFUL LIFE?

The mantra "beauty is pain" is so ingrained into women's collective psyche, we say it to ourselves automatically. As we take off the heels that pinched and bit into our toes, as we hoist up the control-top leggings, or as we gaze longingly at our partner's plate of pancakes while we eat a zero-carb breakfast, we think, "Beauty is pain."

But is that a beautiful life?

Where is the lushness and ease? Where is the self-reverence and gentleness? Where is the confident individuality? Where is the love?

As long as our lives are barren of tenderness and self-love, women are starved for beauty. No number of facial masks or ab workouts will fill that void. Can we enjoy a skincare routine or lose ourselves in the exertion of a cardio class? Sure, but when we're pursuing those activities from a sense of body inadequacy, we'll never achieve the beautiful relief of *enoughness* we're striving for.

George Orwell's classic book *1984* explores the manipulative tactics a totalitarian regime might use to gain mind control over an entire population. In the book, the ruling party uses a series of three slogans, repeated ad nauseam, as part of its rhetoric: "War is peace. Freedom is slavery. Ignorance is strength."

War will never be peace, slavery will never be freedom, ignorance will never be strength.

And pain will never be beauty.

I'm not here to take beauty away from you. I'm here to reconnect you to your natural radiance, to discover the beauty of your True Self, and to help you live a remarkable love story with your body, who is your first and most enduring soulmate.

I'm here to help you discover true beauty.

PART ONE

THE

UNSEEN

STRINGS

---

*The invisible corset is a set of beliefs
that make women as uncomfortable
and restricted in their bodies as
physical corsets once did. We can't cut
the ties of the corset until we identify
and reckon with those strings.*

CHAPTER ONE

BEYOND BODY POSITIVE

Warning! Reflections in this mirror may be distorted by socially constructed ideas of beauty.

—CAPTION FOUND ON A MIRROR DECAL

As women, we consciously and unconsciously measure our bodies against a culturally imposed beauty standard. We internalize this definition of beauty due to the unrelenting barrage of images in media and advertising that perpetuate this standard. Our families and communities, influenced the same way, further ingrain in us appearance-based values. We know this beauty standard is impossible and unrealistic because it's only made possible with Photoshop, professional hair and makeup artists, and cosmetic surgery. We might understand fashion models weigh, on average, 21 percent less than the average woman and that the media's portrayal of the "perfect body" is often a product of severely disordered eating. We may be aware that the beauty industry heavily favors white, Eurocentric faces and severely underrepresents the natural hair, skin tones, and features of women of color. On one level, we realize this beauty standard is toxic and unrealistic. At the same time, we battle our bodies for not conforming to this illusory ideal.

We're all doing our best to navigate this impossible beauty standard. We question aspects of it, yet remain controlled by it. How many of us invest in anti-aging eye creams without asking, "Wait a minute. Why should I spend my money trying to prevent signs of my age?" How many of us automatically reach for the Instagram filters and photo editing apps to smooth our skin without asking, "Why am I photoshopping myself when photoshopped ads have warped my own self-image?" How many of us have studied YouTube tutorials to learn how to fake bigger eyes or deeper cheekbones without wondering, "Why am I trying to make myself look like a different person?"

I used to feel trapped by an illusion of what I believed my body should look like, and that illusion controlled my thoughts and behavior. It was as if I were stuck in a funhouse room of mirrors. I looked at my reflection and saw myself as distorted, instead of realizing the mirrors themselves were warped and misshapen. Instead of leaving the room, I tried to manipulate my body to appear beautiful in those distorted mirrors.

The body positivity movement arose in response to the impossible cultural beauty standard. Through books, documentaries, and social media platforms, this movement seeks to help women love and accept our bodies in a society where billions of advertising dollars are spent to make women hate our appearance. You may have seen before-and-after Photoshop transformation videos on Facebook, showing how digital alterations make the initial model unrecognizable. You may follow Instagram accounts where women post pictures of their cellulite or share a meme stating, "How to have a bikini body: 1. Have a body. 2. Wear a bikini." Perhaps you've noticed corporations riding the wave of body positivity, vowing to avoid retouching models' photos.

Undoubtedly, body positivity has served an immensely positive role, bringing to our awareness the degree of technological, surgical, and cosmetic manipulation behind our cultural beauty standard. But in my experience, body positivity wasn't enough. If it were effective, then I would be able to scroll through my social media feed or flip through a woman's magazine and celebrate my own body, even while confronted with that parade of willowy, poreless, hairless people.

Previously, when I saw body positivity photos or memes in my social media, they only fed into my existing mindset of body comparison and inadequacy. I'd see a celebrity's makeup-free selfie with some wincingly trite caption about embracing one's natural beauty. I'd think, "That's easy for her to say, because she has clear skin instead of the constellation of acne scars I have across my cheeks." Or I'd see an advertisement featuring a curvy model (as in a size 4 rather than a size 0), and I'd think, "She can embrace curvy because her curves are in all the right places, but I gain weight in all the wrong spots."

In my experience, body positivity messages fueled, rather than extinguished, my scathing self-criticism. These messages told me I *should* love my body, but I couldn't. That led me down a mental spiral of guilt and self-blame: I felt searingly insecure about my body, then berated myself for this insecurity. Given the thorough cultural brainwashing we've received, we *should* hate our bodies. It's the only normal—in fact, the only possible—response for women indoctrinated by beauty culture.

Body positivity encourages women to stop comparing our bodies to a beauty standard that is detached from reality because our bodies are beautiful in all shapes, sizes, colors, and conditions. Even if body positivity suggests that different variations of women's bodies are beautiful, it still panders to beauty culture—*the idea that a woman's value is dependent upon whether others perceive her as beautiful.* Expanding the definition of beauty isn't enough; we need to eliminate beauty as a determinant of a woman's worth and societal contribution. Can we still enjoy makeup, skincare, fashion, hairstyling, and other forms of self-adornment and self-expression? Yes! And in fact, we can enjoy beauty accoutrements more when they're not upholding systemic inequality and self-oppression.

WHEN BEAUTY BECOMES BIAS

Makeup isn't a power. Getting dolled up isn't a power.
The lack of need to get dolled up is a power.

—A CAMPUS POSTER created by the
Sookmyung Women's University feminist association

I posted a photo on Instagram, comparing a headshot of myself with makeup and styled hair next to a barefaced photo of myself. In response, one friend told me, "I went to work without makeup one time, and someone asked if I was sick." One of my colleagues replied as well, saying she doesn't normally wear makeup, but "there's this lingering doubt about 'professionalism.' You know, because I get taken more seriously when I wear it." Another friend recounted to me about the time when her manager told her to wear makeup and style her hair, because she would be taken more seriously. All these stories hit home, since my own inner dialogue went along the lines of, "I'll look too young without makeup, and people won't trust my advice." Or, "I won't look professional without makeup." And, "Most people will think I look less attractive without makeup. That surely won't help my career."

This experience is so common, most women don't need proof about it, but research does offer confirmation. One 2011 study suggests that women are seen as more competent, likable, and trustworthy when they wear makeup. Nancy Etcoff, the study's lead author and author of *Survival of the Prettiest*, suggests that women can use this to our advantage. She says, "Twenty or thirty years ago, if you got dressed up, it was simply to please men, or it was something you were doing because society demands it. Women and feminists today see this is their own choice, and it may be an effective tool."

But is it truly a choice if our professional reputation is on the line? Is it fair that going without makeup may harm a woman's career but not a man's? And is it truly an effective tool for professional advancement when it upholds an unfair system, rather than dismantles it?

As of 2019, black men earned an average of eighty-seven cents for every dollar earned by similarly qualified white men in similar jobs. Does this prove that the white men are better at their jobs? Does this mean that if black men wanted to earn more, they should become more white? Of course not! Rather, it suggests a cultural bias that negatively impacts black people. Yet those absurd arguments are employed when it comes to beauty, when people suggest that beauty advantages are biological, and it's "only natural" for women to spend so much time and money on our appearance as a way to increase our success and desirability. A few aspects of what humans consider beautiful do seem to be biological, but by and large, beauty is a social construct determined by cultural, financial, and racist forces (as I'll discuss further in chapter 3). Scholar Tressie McMillan Cottom sums it up when she says, "Beauty isn't actually what you look like; beauty is the preferences that reproduce the existing social order."

In *Survival of the Prettiest*, Etcoff writes:

Women are heavily rewarded for their looks in a way that they are not always rewarded for their other assets, and it is only natural that they put some of their resources into its cultivation. The idea that women would achieve more if they only didn't have to waste time on beauty is nonsense. Women will achieve more when they garner equal legal and social rights and privileges, not when they give up beauty.

But how can we achieve equal rights when we're exhausting our resources on our appearance? Yoon-Kim Ji-Young is a professor at the Institute of Body and Culture at Konkuk University in Seoul. She commented on a feminist movement in South Korea called Escape the Corset. (My jaw dropped to the floor when I learned about this movement after titling this book.) Ji-Young said, "The constant feeling of obsession, self-hatred and fatigue in this competitive society robs us of the energy to address its fundamental, structural inequality."

Various polls reveal that women spend, on average, $225,000 to $300,000 on beauty expenses in their lifetime. Most women aren't spending this money because we enjoy salon visits, hair products, Botox, and makeup *that* much; rather we see them as a means to the ends of success, approval, and romance. Education, mentorship, spiritual development, and relationship coaching might all prove more effective avenues to achieve the business success, self-confidence, and love life we want. Yet we haven't given ourselves the opportunity to realize that because we believe that beauty is our best investment. Since we hold this belief, we've made beauty a profitable self-investment. This is an oppressive social system we unconsciously uphold, *not* our biological fate.

In discussing beauty bias with my friends and colleagues, I've heard variations of the response, "If I didn't capitalize on my appearance, I wouldn't have the success I do," or "I would have better success dating if I was more conventionally beautiful." These statements may indeed be true, but they can also be forms of confirmation bias. This psychological phenomenon occurs when we interpret reality as evidence for our existing beliefs. If our existing beliefs limit us, as in the case of beauty culture, then confirmation bias isn't on our side. Many powerful women chose to believe that it's possible to find legacy, success, and joy while diverging from the beauty standard—and they confirmed that belief! Frieda Kahlo told herself, "I can be an enduring artist without plucking my eyebrows and waxing my upper lip." Lizzo told herself, "I can be an international icon at my current weight." Betty White told herself, "I'll continue my career long after youth fades from my face."

Imagine how different beauty would feel if you *truly* had a choice. You'd be equally confident with and without mascara. You might invite spontaneous and adventurous changes in your appearance, like that haircut you've been secretly considering or a bold fashion choice. Like your male colleagues, you'd feel no need to apologize for not wearing makeup today or for "looking tired." You'd feel no pressure from your job, partner, or social circle to hide your "visible signs of aging." You might feel more confident and uninhibited in your sex life, workplace, and social environment. We can only experience the freedom of beauty when we address the subjugation to it. Then it becomes what we always wanted it to be: fun, celebratory, sensual, and self-expressive.

YOUR RELATIONSHIP TO YOUR BODY IS YOUR RELATIONSHIP TO LIFE

Einstein purportedly said:

The most important question you can ever ask is if the world is a friendly place. For if we decide that the universe is an unfriendly place, then we will use our technology, our scientific discoveries and our natural resources to achieve safety and power by creating bigger walls to keep out the unfriendliness and bigger weapons to destroy all that which is unfriendly. . . . We may either completely isolate or destroy ourselves as well in this process.

We're presently witnessing the manifestation of the concerns in that statement. Humans are on the fast track to cause our own extinction by killing our life-giving planet. We've learned to see the world as a dreadful, threatening place.

The body's intelligence is, of course, an inseparable part of universal intelligence, one of its countless manifestations.

—ECKHART TOLLE

We must also ask ourselves the question, "Is my body a friendly place?" Imagine you're considering the purchase of a new home. One house sits nestled in your ideal environment with blue skies overhead and sweet sunshine filling the air. You open the door, and the space greets you with delight. Even time takes on a different quality here—softer and slower. In this home, colors appear brighter, food tastes better, and your mind feels immediately clearer and expansive. The other home stands in stark contrast, situated in an area with brutally violent weather, like a perpetual Little-House-on-the-Prairie winter. The air in the home feels heavy, as if resentments and bitterness saturate the very walls of the place. In here, your heart races, and you can't catch your breath. Which home would you buy?

The perceptions, beliefs, and expectations we hold of our bodies determine whether we live in that friendly home or the oppressive one. We've tried fruitlessly to change our exterior without addressing the root of the issue, which is how we perceive our bodies. It's like wallpapering the walls of that second house—the energy and the experience remain the same. Fortunately, the biggest and most important relocation of our lives can occur without heavy lifting in the physical world, but simply by a radical shift in our perceptions. This perceptional shift is the most effective, enduring way to transform our physical surroundings.

Botox is the most common form of cosmetic surgery, but it comes with potential side effects ranging from blindness to death. Breast implants place second in the most popular cosmetic surgeries, and these operations frequently come at the price of diminishing or destroying breast and/or nipple sensation. Every day, we reach for makeup and personal care products laden with chemicals, which, when absorbed through the skin after application, are implicated in cancer and auto-immune diseases. Products like skin-bleaching creams and hair relaxers, and procedures such as double-eyelid surgery intended to create a more Eurocentric eye shape, inherently promote a white-supremacist beauty standard. Anorexia, often associated with sociocultural causes, has the highest death rate of any psychiatric illness, including depression. On a less lethal but still disturbing note, the compression garments maker Spanx was valued at a billion dollars in 2012—that's a billion-dollar industry based on restricting women's comfort for the sake of an arbitrary beauty ideal. We are sacrificing our health, our heritage, our sanity, and our *lives* on the altar of our culture's beauty standard not because we choose to, but because we can't see any other choice.

Fear of our own bodies is not a natural state, for it is unnatural to destroy that which gives us joy and pleasure and life. We must ask the question, "Is it a coincidence that women fear their bodies, and as a result we self-destruct? Or is this fear culturally indoctrinated, systematically implemented, and consciously manipulated?" When we examine history and facts, we find this fear is an intentional method of social control to make women fear our bodies. After all, when women are busy destroying ourselves, we're not challenging and fighting the cultural system that oppresses us. Women unlock a triumphant force of creative potential energy when we escape the tunnel vision of body worries.

My body used to be the loneliest, most hostile place I knew. Since it went with me wherever I went, I was perpetually lonely and anxious. Because I was ashamed to be seen with my body, I attracted toxic relationships with people who didn't want to be seen with me. Because I saw my body as unsexy, I gravitated toward experiences that were not sexually fulfilling. Because I thought my health problems meant my body was broken, I didn't create necessary boundaries around other broken, unhealed people. Because I saw my body as never enough, I was magnetized to situations where I was never enough.

I had to learn the truth of women's bodies before I could see myself for who I truly am. This search for truth took me on a journey through history, philosophy, science, medicine, and politics. I discovered that women's self-perception of our bodies has been corrupted by the erasure of history, our lineage of exploitation, and the psychological abuse inherent in beauty culture. I also realized that the truth of women's bodies has been buried, ignored, and decried as blasphemous not by accident, but intentionally. Why? Because this truth is so magnificent and so powerful that it threatens the foundation of hierarchy, violence, and domination upon which our present culture stands.

In order to stop hating our bodies, we need more than a non-photoshopped bikini ad. We need to see the invisible belief systems and power structures that trap women in a hate affair with our bodies.

Only when I saw these invisible restraints, which had been hidden in plain sight, did I recognize the value, worth, and power of my body. I know who my body is, and I am proud to be seen with her. I know her radiance and joy. I know her tremendous capacity to heal. I know her glorious sexuality. I know she offers vast and unique contributions to the world. As a result, my life is now filled with relationships and situations that reflect this awareness.

Are you ready to let the truth of your body set you free?

THE BODY'S WISDOM

If a woman were to trust her body to guide her life, body anxiety would be replaced with awe. But instead of working *with* the force of nature within her body, our culture exerts power *over* her body. We'll never achieve sustainability or relaxation by striving for power *over* nature, only by seeking power with nature.

What is the wisdom written in our bodies? It's the intelligence that guides a fertilized egg to transform into a complex fetus within the womb. It's the internal knowledge directing a child's growth and development. It's the healing power that seals a paper cut and knits back together broken bones in a cast. It's the intuitive compass in your gut.

Our bodies hold the source of our power: our intuition, our creativity, our sexuality. When fully expressed, all these aspects allow a woman to live a life in alignment with her soul, unshackled by societal standards and expectations. She is a seething force of self-confidence requiring permission and acceptance from no one, and her mere presence commands respect from everyone. Women in touch with the wisdom of our bodies are the single greatest threat to societal systems of domination, oppression, and control. We are also the greatest possibility to bring healing, peace, and restoration to our world.

When we control our bodies to fit a beauty standard, we resist the wisdom of nature within us. On a larger scale, that means we resist the force of nature outside of us. As within, so without, as countless mystics have told us. As we learn to trust that divine intelligence within our own bodies, we then work in alignment with the intelligence that animates and informs all the universe. One by one, as women learn to trust their bodies, we will participate in healing the greater body that we are all part of: the Body of Earth.

In order to perpetuate itself, every oppression must corrupt or distort those various sources of power within the culture of the oppressed that can provide energy for change.

—AUDRE LORDE

We've become accomplices to our self-destruction because we haven't been taught to access, recognize, or obey our bodies' vast intelligence. How does this show up? In some cultures, self-destruction is passed from mother to daughter through physical harm. In traditional Chinese culture, mothers were responsible for binding their daughters' feet, leading to excruciating pain and physical handicaps. To this day in many African cultures, older women are responsible for the genital mutilation (clitoris removal) of young girls. Women of the Kayan tribe in Myanmar wrap brass coils around their daughters' necks, which painfully elongates and weakens the neck.

We may consider these destructive practices archaic and barbaric, but the same pattern of destruction occurs in present Western society. Whereas earlier methods of female handicapping were done through physical means, such as foot-binding, it's now accomplished through equally damaging psychological forces. Author Mary Daly, in her book *Gyn/Ecology*, calls it "mind binding." When the brainwashing to destroy our own bodies is thorough enough, physical force is not required. We may not be binding girls' feet, but we are raising them in a culture that curtails their self-confidence and manipulates them to invest an average of $225,000 on beauty in their lifetimes, effectively limiting how far they go in their creativity, careers, and life purpose.

THE INVISIBLE CORSET

Self-hatred is only ever a seed planted from the outside in,
but when you do that to a child, it becomes a weed so thick,
and grows so fast, the child doesn't know any different. . . .
[Self-hatred] becomes as natural as gravity.

—HANNAH GATSBY

The corset has gone through many iterations, but the premise remains the same: it is a restrictive garment that constricts a woman's body into an unnatural shape. It causes constant discomfort and prevents a woman's full movement. Perceived as an essential garment by Western, upper-class women in the nineteenth century, a woman was not fully dressed without it. Women were responsible for inflicting pain on each other, yanking their daughters', sisters', or friends' corsets so tight that the women struggled to catch their breath, were prone to fainting, and were handicapped in their physical movement.

Now that corsets are no longer a normal wardrobe item, we may look back and wonder of our great-grandmothers, "Why did you wear that? Don't you realize you were cutting yourself off from the joy of running and dancing? Didn't you want to breathe easier? Did you realize you were making existence in your body constantly uncomfortable, and you could be more comfortable by simply removing the corset? And, knowing how painful it was, why would you put your daughters in corsets?"

Women discarded their whalebone corsets in the early twentieth century. To the naked eye, it may look like we are now free of that restricting garment. But there remains in place an invisible corset, just as limiting and uncomfortable, and the strings were left in the hands of culture to tighten as it pleased. The invisible corset is a set of beliefs about our bodies that are entirely divorced from reality, just like the sixteen-inch corseted waist is entirely divorced from the reality of a woman's waist. We can't see how these beliefs limit us, restrict us, and make us dependent on a system that is oppressing us. A visible problem proves easier to solve, but invisible restrictions on women are much more insidious.

The cultural beliefs that create the invisible corset make women uncomfortable, restricted, and exhausted in our bodies. *The invisible corset makes us hate our bodies because we hate feeling this way.* Because we've learned to internalize this state as normal and necessary, we unconsciously teach future generations to be uncomfortable, restricted, and exhausted in their bodies as well. We cannot willpower our way out of hating our bodies because we cannot escape something we cannot see. If you want to finally experience peace, comfort, and freedom in your body, you must learn to see the invisible strings.

HOW WE LEARN HATE

On average, a girl's self-confidence starts to decline at age nine and plummets through puberty, as she learns to hate her body and put on the invisible corset. At age nine, I measured my day by the hours spent riding my bike with my friends, not by a number on a scale. I timed how quickly I could run across a soccer field, not the number of eternal minutes spent on a treadmill. I counted the library books I read, not the calories on my dinner plate. I obsessed over how well I could execute a dive at the neighborhood pool, not how my thighs appeared in a bathing suit. At age nine, my body was not a curse but my partner in crime.

Over the next few years, I watched puberty take hold of my peers and leave me, a late bloomer, behind. I felt ashamed, because my body made me acutely different. This sense of being abnormal began to accompany me in every public space, and soon I couldn't even feel relief at home. Suddenly, I became attuned to the comments my mom made about her nose or skin or eyebrows. She was trying to raise a body-confident daughter, commenting on how strong or capable my body was, but a person's energy speaks louder than their words. When a mother carries the energy of body anxiety, it infects her daughters. In addition, I became aware of her dieting. Each time she condemned an item of food as "bad" or "too high in calories," I internalized fear toward that particular food or ingredient and tried to avoid it. These dieting lessons, coupled with a desperate need to feel control over my life, threw me into a spiral of extreme anorexia by the time I was eleven.

The larger world never gives girls the message that their bodies are valuable simply because they are inside them.

—NAOMI WOLF

Even though I grew up in a highly media-censored household, without cable TV and with strict internet limits, I still absorbed marketing messages about my body. As I walked through the supermarket aisles, beauty products promised to "fix," "repair," "boost," and "smooth" me. As a result, I believed I could buy inner radiance, confidence, and self-esteem. Whereas I'd previously spent my piggy bank change on craft supplies and cookbooks, I now spent my babysitting money at Sephora, buying a "holy grail" product that would make existence in my body more tolerable. My preoccupation with changing my body meant I stopped creating, and my crafts, hobbies, and projects halted. Even with pricey skin creams and cosmetics, the boost in confidence was like a drug high—lasting only a moment, and requiring a greater investment the next time. There was nowhere I could go to escape my self-loathing. Alone in my bedroom, I was surrounded by beauty products that clamored, "You are not enough without me, and even I am not enough to fix you."

Everything and everyone taught me how to hate my body, but no one taught me how to undo this hatred. I had unwittingly put on the invisible corset and didn't know how to take it off. Instead of trying to return to the easy partnership I once felt with my body, I spent much of my trying to hate her better. I learned how to override her hunger and thirst signals and to better follow the diet rules laid out for me in magazines. I learned how to silence her fatigue so I could achieve school and work accomplishments at the expense of my health. I learned to numb the pain of my own abusive dialogue toward my body. I learned to join other women in conversations where we criticized our own bodies. I learned to forget feeling free in my body.

As soon as women learn to hate our bodies, our existence becomes a chore of conformity rather than a joy of self-expression. Simone de Beauvoir said, "To lose confidence in one's body is to lose confidence in oneself." Instead of teaching girls how to expand their confidence and self-expression, we are passing down the invisible corset from mother to daughter. We are perpetuating a history of bondage rather than a legacy of freedom. Now, women are tasked with a great unlacing of the corset strings that make us hate our bodies and our lives.

THE CURSE OF DISFIGUREMENT

In the old French fairy tale "Beauty and the Beast," Beauty discovers her father is being held hostage by a treacherous and hideous Beast. To save her father, Beauty chooses to take his place in the Beast's estate. The Beast ensures Beauty lives in luxury at his home, and they dine together each evening. At the end of each evening, he asks her, "Beauty, will you marry me?" Beauty responds each time, "No Beast, I do not love you."

When Beauty's father falls ill, Beast grants her a return visit back home. "But return to me, Beauty, for I love you," Beast says. At home, she tells her sisters of the luxury that surrounds her at the estate. Jealous, they attempt to drug her into a deep sleep. Beauty wakes up from a long sleep, in which she dreams Beast lies dying in his garden. Upon waking, she runs back to his estate and finds him in the garden, barely breathing.

"Beast, do not die!" she cries, flinging herself on him.

"Will you marry me now, Beauty?" Beast says.

"Yes, Beast, for I love you and cannot live without you."

With those words, she watches Beast transform into a handsome prince. "You loved me while I was ugly, and so doing released me from my curse," Beast says. "I was condemned by a fairy to be a repulsive beast until someone loved me enough to marry me." As Beast was transformed, so were the many servants at the estate, who had also fallen under the curse of the fairy and made invisible. They now joyfully found themselves in their bodies again. Beauty's love was so potent it even changed her selfish sisters, who became kind and generous.

You are the best thing to ever happen to you.

—ANDREA GIBSON

Like the Beast, women's bodies have fallen under the curse of disfigurement. Instead of an evil fairy, however, culture is responsible for cursing women's bodies as unintelligent, unattractive, and altogether unworthy of love. As long as the curse remains in place, women will feel trapped by their bodies, just like Beauty felt trapped by the Beast. All the while, our bodies generously offer us everything we need for our lives, just like the Beast spread a nightly feast for Beauty.

We have two choices. We can feel trapped by our bodies, wearing the invisible corset, and pass this curse down from generation through generation, or we can learn to see our bodies as who they truly are: not Beasts, but our beloved and beautiful partners. When we do that, we transform not only our own bodies but also every other woman's body, just like Beauty's love transformed her sisters. For when one woman learns to love her body, she frees other women to do the same.

EXERCISE: Losing Your Best Friend

In the following exercise, you'll recall the separation from your body. Open your fresh journal for this first exercise.

Start with the following prompt:

> *Dear Body,*
> *I remember how close you and I were. But I learned that I*
> *wasn't safe with you, and that I shouldn't be your friend.*
> *I learned that it wasn't okay to love you.*

Now, you'll practice something called speed writing, a writing technique that allows you to tap your subconscious mind for insight, meaty truth, and repressed memories. For this technique, you must keep your pen moving across the paper. The key is to write faster than your inner critic can respond, spilling out words before hesitation holds them back. The purpose is to write usefully, not beautifully. Ignore any concerns you may have with spelling, grammar, or punctuation. This is a practice in radical self-honesty.

Set a timer for seven minutes and, after writing the prompt down in your journal, speed write anything that comes up. How did you learn your body was to be feared? When did you divorce your body? Why?

Then, after the timer rings, close by writing the following:

> *In the past, I've hurt you, physically and verbally. I tried to*
> *escape and replace you. I tried to make you look and act like*
> *someone else. Please know, it was never about you.*

I was trying my best to survive in a world that convinced
me you were my liability, instead of my true love.
I miss you. I miss loving you. I want to be friends again.
Love,
[Your Name]

This letter marks the beginning of the journey you'll take through this book to reconnect with your lifelong partner: your body.

CHAPTER TWO

FEAR

In Victorian times, it was not considered ladylike for a woman to have sexual desire or enjoyment. So women feared and, therefore, repressed their sexuality. However, it was socially acceptable for a woman to go to a doctor's office and pay for medical treatment where a doctor stimulated her to orgasm. (The first vibrators were designed for medical offices.) It wasn't for pleasure; it was a medical treatment for "hysteria." This official diagnosis required a doctor's assistance and profited the medical industry.

This technique proved so effective and lucrative that the beauty and diet industries appear to have taken note. Simply make the normal experience of a woman's body a problem, withhold education on how she can feel better naturally and easily, and then sell her a solution. Voilà! The fear of her natural body creates an instant and dependent customer.

THE FACES OF FEAR

In order to solve a problem, we have to first accurately identify what it is. Women hate our bodies; and the root of all hate is fear. We have a fear problem, not a hate problem.

Fear of our bodies is not a natural state, but a learned phenomenon. When we don't understand someone's language or values, we often interpret that difference as them being wrong and us being right. Instead of celebrating diversity as a way to widen our perspective, we've learned to hate difference because it threatens our limited perceptions. Fear of another person leads us to cut them off and blame them rather than communicate and empathize with them. The same phenomenon occurs with our bodies: we fear our bodies because we do not understand their language and values. This fear is the first corset string.

Diversity is strength. Difference is a teacher.
Fear difference, you learn nothing.

—HANNAH GATSBY

We face two choices when we are afraid of our bodies. First, we can try to control them through force and domination. This approach inevitably requires violence and self-bullying, prevents self-love, and perpetuates the misunderstandings we hold of our bodies. This creates a cycle of disconnection, establishing a never-ending war between ourselves and our bodies, which we perceive as the enemy. The invisible corset traps us into this self-battle, so we exhaust our energies repressing ourselves instead of channeling that energy to express ourselves.

Our second option is to trust our bodies through communication and empathy. When trust is present in a relationship, control and domination are not needed. Trust manifests naturally from a state of connection with our bodies, whereas control arises when we are disconnected from them. Trust is a state of *being* fueled by love, whereas control is a state of *doing* driven by fear.

The corset string of fear sabotages women's time, energy, and happiness to the degree we fail to recognize it. In order to begin the unlacing, we must see the ways we've been taught to be afraid of our bodies.

Women Are Afraid of Body Fat

I once started each day reading my belly's bad news. I'd stand sideways in front of the bathroom mirror, scrutinizing the curve below my belly button. On good days, my stomach looked acceptably small. When I perceived myself as bloated or heavier, I started my day telling myself, "I need to fix my body today. I need to get back on track. I need to disguise my shape with clothing." I swallowed my shame, anger, and despair, then faced the day ahead.

We've accepted the belief that thinness makes us beautiful, successful, lovable, desirable. But if we examine that definition of desirability, we realize that it's our pain, weakness, and controllability that is desired. A woman who is afraid of fat is easily manipulated and kept under control. In fact, corrupt authority figures, abusive partners, and profit-hungry industries define desirability in such a way as to control your behavior. It's an age-old technique!

In her bestselling book *The Beauty Myth*, Naomi Wolf shares critical historical insight about why culture seeks to control women's weight. The ultrathin, boyish flapper aesthetic came into style shortly after women tossed aside their handicapping physical corsets and gained the right to vote. As most women require diligent dieting to obtain that body type, women were now burdened with a task that diverted their attention away from political liberation. There is nothing more mentally, emotionally, and psychically depleting than following a diet—but only the women who stop dieting realize this. Otherwise, many of us go through our lives believing eating is inevitably fraught with anxiety and obsession.

Dieting, defined by restricting caloric intake to induce weight loss, may be the least effective way to maintain a stable weight or long-term health. Not only do most individuals regain the lost weight after dieting, but 30 to 60 percent of them also gain *more* weight, since dieting effectively lowers one's metabolic rate. Those individuals never failed the diets; the mythical concept of an "effective diet" failed them. Those who are lean to begin with, rather than obese, may face the biggest risks: they're likely to gain more weight with continued yo-yo dieting, and this may also increase the risk of type 2 diabetes and high blood pressure for those with "normal" body mass indexes (BMIs).

Further, overeating is often *caused* by dieting. In their landmark book *Intuitive Eating*, nutritionists Evelyn Tribole and Elyse Resch explain that the mere perception of food deprivation and the concept of forbidden foods typically trigger binging. They call this Last Supper eating. "The overeating that [occurs when one slips up on a diet or decides to start a new diet] falsely gives 'proof' that you need to diet, as you watch in horror your inability to 'control' yourself." Feeling out of control around food is the result of a diet mindset, not an indication of the necessity of food rules. As Caroline Dooner, an author and anti-diet advocate says, "Lots of people think they're addicted to food, but they are actually addicted to dieting." When we pit our willpower against our bodies' evolutionary wisdom, our bodies win.

The health dangers of dieting infect our children as well. Many of my clients tell me they learned to diet by observing their mothers' food habits and weight anxiety, and I share this experience as well. Mothers who talk about their weight, shape, or size are more likely to have daughters with lower self-esteem. Their daughters are also more likely to report feelings of depression and use dangerous weight control methods like binging or purging, or using diuretics and laxatives. To be comfortable in my body, I had to undo generations of diet consciousness that was embedded in my mind. What if we broke the cycle so our daughters could channel their energies into avenues of pleasure, joy, and rest, instead of 24/7 diet duties?

If the fact that *dieting can make you fatter and can handicap your daughters* isn't enough to encourage a different relationship with food, consider also the impacts on mental health. Every day I help clients who struggle with food obsession. If they're not berating themselves for what they ate, they're planning their next meal, researching nutrition, or preparing for their next diet. Often, they give food more consideration, planning, and priority than their spouses or partners. They thought food would solve their body insecurity problems, but food has become their biggest problem. "I just want to eat normally," they tell me, "but I don't know how to stop this obsession." No matter how fraught your relationship with food is, it *is* possible to eat normally and trust yourself around food. (If you'd like further support with this, check out my Food without Fear program in the resources section.)

You might be wondering, "But isn't weight loss important for health?" Actually, we have no conclusive research showing that body fat directly causes disease, although a correlation has been shown. Research also shows that higher levels of body fat correlate to a longer life and longer survival for many diseases. Further, when we keep our focus on weight loss, we miss the other avenues that can improve our health. For example, loneliness can be a more significant factor in health than obesity, smoking, exercise, or nutrition. Literature suggests that genetics and personal health choices account for only 25 percent of one's health status—the remaining 75 percent is due to socioeconomic status, environment, and health care. To change the systemic roots of poor health, we need to get off the hamster wheel of dieting.

Thinness isn't a cure.

—ANNA SWEENEY

The Association for Size Diversity and Health raises the following question: If weight loss doesn't necessarily improve health, and yo-yo dieting is associated with negative health issues, is it ethical to encourage people to lose weight? That's the $72 billion question.

In 2017, the diet industry was valued at $72 billion. It has created a lucrative cycle, offering an addictive, short-term high that keeps people coming back for more, all the while sabotaging their physical and mental health. The research suggesting that dieting threatens our health certainly challenges conventional medical advice, and this wouldn't be the first or the last time that conventional knowledge fails our wellbeing. Consider that, in the mid-1980s, mainstream science told us butter caused heart attacks, and we should eat more margarine and carbs. The American public adopted the advice and rates of heart disease, stroke, diabetes, and chronic illness skyrocketed. Thirty years later, as *Time* magazine reported in 2014, we realized that dietary fat was never the enemy. Instead of fearing body fat, we should be more afraid of inaccurate research.

Our culture's fear of body fat is not a statement of health and wellness, it's the internalized fear of our own freedom. Does this mean we should never strive to lose weight? It means we should examine the motivations behind wanting to lose weight. If you want to lose weight to be beautiful, it's critical to understand your concept of beauty is conflated with social control mechanisms intended to make you afraid of *you*. It's much easier to siphon your finances and mental energy when you don't trust your body. Also, body weight naturally and healthfully varies, just like height. If you want to lose weight to be healthy, it's critical to understand body fat can be *a symptom* of underlying health imbalances, but it isn't a disease in and of itself. Trying to solve the symptom through losing weight rather than gaining health, may harm your health. If you want to lose weight to be more confident, energetic, active, or sexually expressive, make those your goals, not weight loss. Overeating can also be an emotional coping mechanism, but it's much more effective to address the underlying emotional issues or trauma that led to that coping mechanism. This is one area of focus when I work with clients around food issues. As modern-day mystic Charles Eisenstein says, "Rather than take away someone's medicine, instead remove the conditions that make the medicine necessary."

Women Are Afraid of Body "Imperfections"

Before the word *cellulite* was invented in the late 1900s, it was simply normal female flesh. There's nothing intrinsically wrong with cellulite. Although it can sometimes indicate a congestion of lymphatic fluid, cellulite is not inherently ugly or unhealthy. Historically, full and dimpled flesh has been considered beautiful and enviable in Western culture—just Google "Peter Paul Rubens art" for proof. Selling "treatments" for cellulite is, in fact, simply creating a cellulite problem.

We witness the same pattern of inventing a problem with the normal female body when we see body hair, under-eye circles, and visible pores as problematic. In an Instagram Story video, author Glennon Doyle discussed a realization that hit her one morning when she was applying concealer under her eyes. She asked herself, "Why am I trying to hide the circles under my eyes? Being a woman is exhausting!"

In April 1968, Vogue *became the first English-language periodical to print the term "cellulite," engendering both a new word and a fashionable new way for American women to hate their bodies.*

—KELSEY MILLER

The beauty industry insists we must mask and disguise certain aspects of our bodies. But these are not imperfections or failures, they are the truth of our lives. Shaming a woman's body isn't about her body, it's about shaming her life and her experiences. Underlying every body-shaming statement is the message, "You are existing in the wrong way."

Our culture's glorification of thinness is not about beauty because a "beautiful weight" is a cultural construct. In the same way, our culture's obsession with cosmetics is not about beauty but about instilling fear for financial control. Consider the belief that our faces need to be "corrected" by makeup. Curiously, this correction often means making a woman look less like herself and more like someone else. The fad of contouring, for example, rests on the concept that women look better with thinner noses, higher cheekbones, and sharper jawlines. These alterations do not make a woman look biologically *better*; they make her look different. (I'll further address the "it's biology" argument about beauty in chapter 3.)

Modern makeup trends include more steps and products than ever before, and not because they make us more beautiful. The more makeup we can layer on our face, the more tools and applicators required, the more money we spend on cosmetics. Betty Friedan's book *The Feminine Mystique* discusses how the culture of the early 1960s idealized a woman's homemaking. She wrote, "Why is it never said that the really crucial function, the really important role that women serve as housewives is to *buy more things for the house*" (emphasis mine). In the same way, the role women play as beauty objects is *to buy more things for our face and bodies*.

While there is a degree of marketing-based manipulation here, there is, perhaps, also a need fulfilled. I used to confuse my beauty routine with self-care. For example, I elevated my intricate skin-care routine to a nearly sacred level and told myself this was about my wellness, not about my desire to conform to a beauty standard. Later, I realized that my skincare routine fulfilled a deeper need: undisturbed time dedicated to myself, without feeling guilty about it. Women often feel guilty for taking time for themselves, except when it comes to beauty, and this, again, is cultural orchestration rather than coincidence. The beauty industry doesn't want women to feel guilty for spending time and money on themselves if it means we're buying more products, so the beauty industry tells us that *we're worth it* and *we deserve it*. When I understood that my beauty routine wasn't self-care but an excuse to enjoy myself without guilt, I could let go of the excuse.

I considered other ways I could provide myself with quality "me" time. For example, I started taking solo neighborhood walks without my phone, picked up playing the piano again, and read more fiction books. I decided I would reject feelings of guilt for spending quality time with myself, recognizing that this emotion was merely an automatic response programmed by my culture's commercialism. My favorite definition of self-care is creating a life you don't routinely have to escape. By that definition, true self-care means escaping from the invisible corset, not using complex skincare routines to conform to industry-established beauty standards. Skincare can be a self-reverent, relaxing experience, but only if we've released fears of body inadequacy and aging. Body fear and relaxed self-reverence don't coexist.

Additionally, due to the time required for their application, complex cosmetic routines serve an invisible and oppressive social function. The time most women spend researching, shopping for, and applying makeup is time not spent on our education, self-growth, or career. For many women, cosmetics provide a creative outlet in much the same way that needlepoint and handiwork did in the Victorian era. The embroidery created by Victorian women was truly art—an expression of both great creativity and skill—and it was also a form of non-socially-disruptive art that kept women in their place, as Wolf explains in *The Beauty Myth*. Women have such potent and vast creative energy that society attempts to provide us with nondisruptive outlets for this energy. Yes, makeup can be a powerful tool for artistic self-expression. But on the whole, the cosmetic industry—and the cosmetic surgery industry—has done more to strip women's confidence than to boost it. When we feel imperfect without makeup, applying it doesn't make us more confident. Concealer can't fix insecurity, it just temporarily covers it up. If our bodies change, but our minds remain the same, our bodies will never make us happy. As I cut the invisible corset strings, my relationship to makeup shifted. Now when I look in the mirror, I appreciate my face and find her worthy of adorning, but I'm also comfortable going without makeup. In fact, I prefer it because I don't worry that I'm deceiving people about the truth of my body, or fear someone seeing me without it. Sometimes, I struggle with lingering insecurity about my makeup-free face. But when that body-fearing emotion arises, I remind myself that the truth of my body isn't capable of making me less-than, because it's what makes me *me*.

Women Are Afraid of Race and Ethnicity

In a viral social media video, a woman is doing the hair of a four-year-old black girl, when the little girl says, "I so ugly." The woman gasps, and replies with conviction, "Don't say that. Don't say that! You are so pretty." The woman points out the girl's dimples and chocolate skin, but the girl starts sobbing. A tear slips down the woman's face as she holds the girl, saying, "Baby girl, you are beautiful. Black is beautiful."

I talk to many white women, clients and friends alike, who tell me the heartbreak they felt when their little girls made their first body-hating comment. Helpless and horrified, they watched their daughters' minds become poisoned by beauty culture. It is heartbreaking. Even more heartbreaking is that black and brown little girls have it worse. White women receive the cultural message that they have to be beautiful to be worthy, and they fundamentally fall short of beauty. Women of color receive the additional message: "You have to be white to be worthy, and you fundamentally fall short of whiteness." That is the ideology of white supremacy, upon which Western culture was built and still exists.

If you are white, were you ever successful in convincing yourself that your cellulite or acne was beautiful? If you're like me, no. That's because the existence of anti-cellulite products and photoshopped models led you to believe beauty excludes dimpled or marked skin. In the same way, the existence of skin-lightening creams and hair relaxers convey the message that beauty excludes black or brown features and skin. Beauty culture upholds racism, just as it upholds sexism. Culture insists something is wrong with women's natural bodies in order to make them profitable and less powerful. Culture insists something is wrong with black bodies in order to make them profitable and less powerful.

Many people consider racism a bias held by mean, ignorant people. In reality, it's an often unconscious prejudice reinforced by systems of power. In her book *So You Want to Talk About Race*, author Ijeoma Oluo explains, "Systemic racism is a machine that runs whether we pull the levers or not, and by just letting it be, we are responsible for what it produces. We have to actually dismantle the machine if we want to make change." We have much work to do, but by dismantling beauty culture, we dismantle one cog of systemic racism.

Some corporations make a show of body positivity, featuring plus-size models and vowing abstinence from retouching. Their intention is largely commercial rather than altruistic, since they extend body positivity only so far as it is the most profitable stance. If truly committed to body acceptance, they would no longer hire models with disordered eating habits or who had undergone plastic surgery. They would no longer peddle dangerous detox products and diets. They would no longer sell anti-aging or anti-cellulite products. They would ensure that body, skin tone, and facial diversity in their advertising reflected the global population to which they market.

Just as with body positivity, some beauty companies make a nice show at racial diversity. They may feature a model of color or expand the number of foundation shades they offer. This may seem like a step forward, but it can distract consumers from the bigger change that's needed. For example, in 2017, L'Oréal fired a mixed-race, transgender model after she discussed systemic racism in a personal Instagram post. The corporation backtracked on equality as soon as the manifestation of it led to controversy and threatened industry profits. To truly walk their talk, beauty companies—particularly white-owned companies—must hire, educate, and fund the change they want to see in the world.

Women Are Afraid of Aging

When women around me comment that their gray roots are showing, I've started to pipe up with, "I can't wait until I have silver moonlight gleaming in my hair!" Whenever a woman criticizes her wrinkles or aging body in public, my first thought is, "Someone's daughter heard that. Maybe many daughters heard that. Why are we telling them that age is something to hide and fear?"

Our culture seeks to repress women's power through youth glorification. Many women spend their money, time, and energy to fight the visible signs of aging with skincare, makeup, and cosmetic surgery. We unquestioningly accept the cultural myth that youth is beauty, but actually, the truth of ourselves is beauty because that's where our power and confidence resides. It is no coincidence that the beauty standard portrayed in the media is of a young, sometimes prepubescent, girl who has not lived long enough to step into her power or to accumulate the wisdom of decades. A woman's potential intuitive, sexual, and financial power increases with age. The extreme double standard in "acceptable aging" for men and women illustrates our culture's repression of female power. A man who is gray at the temples is dignified, while a woman has let herself go.

My face carries all my memories. Why would I erase them?

—DIANE VON FURSTENBERG

One argument used to defend culture's obsession with female youth is that it's evolutionary for men to desire younger women because they are more fertile. This "biology argument" falls apart at the seams when examined. Our beauty standard is a young woman model who is, on average, seventeen years old. Many models are younger, still prepubescent at fourteen, and not yet fertile, so they are not viable mates according to the biology theory. Many models and actresses achieve their low weight through disordered eating. This has a negative impact on their sex hormones, and may even cause their period to cease—again, making them an inopportune for furthering a man's DNA. A woman's fertility peaks between the ages of twenty and twenty-four, and tends to noticeably decline at age thirty-five, so a rail-thin woman of seventeen is certainly not in her fertile prime.

Further, the biology argument fails to justify the use of cosmetic surgery, such as Botox and face-lifts. These procedures are used to fake youthful looks, which would supposedly make women more attractive. But our bodies are smarter than that.

Dr. Stephen Porges, a leading researcher on the intersection of neuroscience and evolutionary biology, established the polyvagal theory.

This theory covers many aspects of human connectivity and empathy, but here's what you need to know regarding our topic of anti-aging cosmetic surgery.

The vagal nerve is the wiring that connects our brain and many organs in the body. The vagal nerve activates when we're feeling happy and relaxed, and this correlates to the muscles around our eyes crinkling with expression. This change is subtle but is subconsciously registered by other people. That's because the nervous system picks up information at a rate much faster than the conscious awareness. So when someone has this subtle crinkling around their eyes as they talk and smile, we subconsciously feel safe around them.

You may have noticed that you feel vaguely unsettled when conversing with someone whose facial muscles have limited mobility due to Botox or surgery. This is because your nervous system may be communicating to you, "I'm not receiving an evolutionary message of safety from their facial expressions." Anti-aging cosmetic work may make someone more attractive according to our cultural beauty standard, but this attraction is at a conscious level. At a subconscious, biological level, we may feel less drawn to them because their facial microexpressions are restricted.

Our culture has taught us to fear showing the story of our lives on our faces and bodies. Women's magazines perpetually tout headlines such as "How to Prevent Stretch Marks!" and "Get Your Pre-Baby Body Back!" As women, we often fail to question why we should hide our life experiences from our bodies. Wouldn't erasing the marks of childbirth, marks that provide visible testament to the life-giving power of a woman's body, decrease, rather than increase, the value of her body? Our bodies show the stories of our lives. We live in a culture, however, that seeks to rewrite women's true experience not only in our history books but also on our bodies.

Women Are Afraid of Our Emotions

When I struggled with a chronic disease, I used to think my autoimmune symptoms were the problem. Then I realized, instead of being the problem, those symptoms were messages telling me how I needed to adjust my nutrition, stress levels, expectations of my life, and even my spiritual beliefs. Those symptoms weren't what I needed to change; they revealed the perspectives and situations I needed to change. In the same way, we often fear negative emotions when they are the valuable (albeit painful) information we need to solve the real problem.

Emotions such as chronic unhappiness, anger, apathy, grief, and anxiety are the equivalent of a smoke detector's alarm going off. The alarm doesn't indicate something is wrong with the smoke detector; it indicates there is smoke and fire in the environment. Viktor Frankl, the holocaust survivor who wrote *Man's Search for Meaning*, said, "An abnormal reaction to an abnormal situation is a normal reaction." The one in four women prescribed antidepressants in the United States aren't having abnormal emotional responses; they're having normal emotional reactions to an abnormal cultural environment and its abnormal expectations.

[Depression] is an adaptive response, intelligently communicated by the body, to something not being right within, often because things are also off in our environment.

—KELLY BROGAN

Is it possible that common psychotropic drugs are sometimes necessary and often helpful? I'm inclined to believe so, based on personal anecdotes that have been shared with me. However, the imbalanced brain-chemical theory upon which antidepressant use is predicated has never been proved. When non-industry-funded research is taken into consideration, the most common form of antidepressants (SSRIs, or selective serotonin reuptake inhibitors) are not more effective than placebos. Chronic inflammation is actually a leading physiological cause of depression, and inflammation is environmental—largely created by our nutrition and lifestyle. In addition, anxiety and depression are normal responses to a culture that breeds terror of our own bodies, chronic self-loathing, perpetual people pleasing, disconnection from nature, and repression of our intuition.

Many mental health practitioners would agree that it's appropriate to first determine if a woman is in an abusive relationship before prescribing her antidepressants or antianxiety drugs. Otherwise, the practitioner runs the risk of increasing her tolerance to a dangerous, and sometimes life threatening, situation. In the same way, practitioners should determine if these drugs are appropriate when a woman is in an abusive relationship with her cultural situation. As I'll discuss in chapter 6, beauty culture employs the same tactics as a psychologically abusive partner and creates the same type of harm.

Our emotions aren't something to fear because they show us the way out: out of the beliefs, expectations, relationships, and environments that cause us pain. And ultimately, our emotions show us the way out of beauty culture.

Women Are Afraid of Their Authentic Sexuality

My high heels clicked across the floor as I walked from the restaurant table to the restroom. "Is sexiness supposed to feel so uncomfortable?" I wondered.

It was my twenty-third birthday, and my date had taken me to a downtown restaurant to celebrate. I hadn't eaten carbs for a week, so my stomach was flat enough for the skin-tight dress he had given me. It was cut so low, I was afraid to bend over. My breasts were crammed impossibly close to my collarbones in a push-up bra. His eyes followed me as I walked, a gaze that felt hungry and vaguely dangerous. I noticed other men's heads swivel away from their dinner companions toward me. If I caught their eyes, I looked immediately to the floor.

I couldn't breathe fully. I couldn't move fully. If this was what sexy felt like, then why did I want to crawl out of my skin? Why did I want to cry?

At the time, I didn't know that being desired isn't the same as being valued. I didn't know that the cultural sexual aesthetic might not match with my personal sexual expression. And no one told me that if I released myself from culturally defined expectations of sexy, the freedom and pleasure I could experience would be one of the most powerful dispelling forces of the body insecurities I faced.

Sex is one of the most interesting things we as humans have to play with, and we've reduced it to polyester underpants and implants. We are selling ourselves unbelievably short.

—ARIEL LEVY

As with many women, my psyche was imprinted with conflicting messages about sex. On the one hand, I grew up with the sexual repression enforced by purity culture, and the lack of body and pleasure education made me vulnerable to toxic sexual dynamics as a young adult. On the other hand, the media told me that a woman's sexiness is determined by her appearance and her ability to provide pleasure and an ego boost for her partner. This media message also largely disregarded a woman's pleasure and self-expression, and focused on the degree to which others perceive her as desirable.

The porn industry, like the beauty industry, presents a very narrow spectrum of women's bodies, preferences, and pleasure preferences. The sexual narrative perpetuated by that industry can lead women to internalize fear-based beliefs about our bodies, in the form of the following narratives.

- Sexy is a prescribed *appearance* for a woman, not an *experience* of her body.

- Men are entitled to sexual pleasure at the expense of a woman's physical, emotional, or psychological comfort.

- Women are grateful after they are forced or coerced into sexual acts, and any pleasure they experience somehow excuses their sexual assault.

- Female sexuality should look like that depicted in pornography. If a woman's sexuality, including how she reaches orgasm or what she feels comfortable doing in bed, doesn't match pornography, then: a) her body is wrong, b) she is doing something wrong, or c) she's not sexual enough.

Rather than showing the true spectrum of a woman's sexual enjoyment, in order to create the most profitable imagery, porn typically shows actresses *imitating* sexual pleasure and/or enduring pain. In a culture obsessed with *looking* sexy, women are often unable to *feel* sexy. We have confused other people's approval of our bodies with sexual enjoyment of our bodies. A prime example manifests in the skyrocketing rates of breast implants and labiaplasty (cosmetic surgery of the labia). Women often say they are choosing to undergo these surgeries so they can "feel sexy." "It's for their own confidence, and not to gain anyone else's approval," they may say.

But why would a woman feel more sexy after getting implants, when these surgeries frequently cause desensitization of her erotic breast tissue and even nipple numbness? In the same way, labiaplasty also carries the side effect of desensitization of highly erotic tissue. Too often, women confuse *appearing* sexy or *performing* sexy with feeling sexy. When sexiness is defined as a woman's own experience of erotic pleasure, these surgeries are more likely to reduce, instead of increase, her sexiness.

Women's sexual liberation must not be confused with our cultural commercialization of women's bodies. Brazilian waxes aren't inherently sexy (although they are inherently painful). They're an aesthetic designed to create profits for the diet and porn industries. Similarly, flat stomachs or dimple-free thighs aren't inherently sexy; they are an aesthetic peddled by the diet and liposuction industries.

Sex does sell—when advertisers convince women that the sexual pleasure and erotic intimacy we crave is on the other side of body modification.

After leaving the man I dated in my early twenties, I read a book in which a woman described the most intense sexual pleasure she'd ever experienced. The rapture was so unrelenting, she thought she was going to die from a heart attack. She didn't discuss the lingerie she might have been wearing, or the false eyelashes and highlighter she might have worn, or if she had lost weight to achieve that experience. She didn't report that she earned this pleasure through beauty labor, but instead focused on the absolute gift of her body and her self-knowledge for making that experience possible.

After reading, I thought, "Dear God, I want that." Soon, I'd find myself in a profoundly healing and awakening sexual relationship. For the first time, I experienced ecstasy so overpowering, it felt like instantaneous death was a viable possibility. At the time, I was makeup-free, had long since disposed of all my underwire bras, and had definitely been eating carbs. That's what sexy can look like. In fact, orgasmic pleasure provides an accessible and powerful way to start focusing on your body as a being rather than an object. But there's often a catch-22, as I've realized both with myself and my clients. Body insecurities and orgasm anxiety ("Am I going to come? Am I taking too long? Is my partner getting bored or tired?") can prevent the relaxation and receptivity essential to profound pleasure. To facilitate this shift out of your head and into your body, see the resources section for some tools and techniques to use by yourself or with a partner.

Women Are Afraid of Their Intuition

We have been trained to reject our inner voice—our intuition—and instead outsource responsibility for our wellbeing to industries and experts. Although we hear the trite advice to follow your intuition, the barrage of marketing messages we hear really tell us to trust anyone but ourselves. "Don't trust your hunger, follow this diet!" "Don't trust your fatigue, drink coffee!" "Don't trust your anxiety, drink wine!" "Don't trust your spiritual curiosity, curb your doubt!"

One reason we hesitate to listen to our intuition is because it's culturally shamed. We live in a society that glorifies empirical data. We're taught to make our life choices based on analytical decision-making, arriving at decisions based on analysis of available, measurable data. Our decisions are supposed to be based on past patterns and historical information. Most of all, our decisions are supposed to make sense to other people.

> *That is the real power of intuition—that it gives us,*
> *at every moment, the capacity to change our destiny.*
> —MONA LISA SCHULZ

In a workshop, author Elizabeth Gilbert told a story about her colleague, a famed TV interviewer. The interviewer asked many renowned women, "How did you achieve your success?" On camera, the women offered responses that made logical sense, things along the lines of, "I worked hard, I persevered, I took risks." When the camera turned off, many of the same women turned to the interviewer and said in hushed tones, "You know what it really was?" Then, they would say, "I got insight from a dream," or "I just had this gut feeling." These powerful, successful women weren't comfortable publicly admitting they made life-altering choices based on their intuition alone.

Our culture leads women to fear intuitive decision-making because it doesn't make sense, it's not measurable, and it's not provable. All of that is true, and so is this: intuition works. The invisible corset cuts us off from our bodies' wisdom, the source of our intuition and inner guidance. As you remove the corset through the exercises in this book, you'll turn up the volume on your intuition and gather the courage to make choices that set you on your most fulfilling life path.

FEARING BIGGER

In September 2019, Demi Lovato posted a photo on her Instagram page, striking a power pose in her bikini as she stepped out of a pool. The caption said, "This is my biggest fear. A photo of me in a bikini unedited." In the rest of the caption, she celebrated her body and new-found body authenticity. Upon reading it, I appreciated Demi's courage and honesty. I applauded that she posted the truth of her body while afraid. But I also felt distress that the greatest fear of any woman is showing up in her body, in the world, without editing.

Body fear traps women in the invisible corset, limiting our ability to eat normally, age with power, trust our emotions, make intuitive choices, and spend our money and energy where it truly counts. Let's fear bigger and bolder: let our biggest fear be not expressing our voices, our creativity, and our dreams. Let us fear not living our lives fully, pleasurably, and exuberantly.

CHAPTER THREE

DOMINATION

*Violence is first of all authoritarian. It begins
with this premise: I have the right to control you.*

—REBECCA SOLNIT

No matter how many affirmations I repeated, social media posts I
bookmarked, or how many self-love books I read, I couldn't force myself
to accept my body. That's because loving our bodies is not a result of
willpower, but a matter of learning the truth of our bodies. Western
culture teaches us we have the right to dominate our bodies because
they are things we own rather than beings with whom we are in relationship. This is the second corset string: relating to our bodies through
domination.

OWNERSHIPS VS. PARTNERSHIPS

Domination creates *ownerships* of our bodies instead of supportive
partnerships with them. In an ownership, we hold the expectation
that the other is obligated to fulfill our needs. We feel entitled to this
individual behaving and speaking in a way that makes our own life
convenient and comfortable. We fail to realize that the other person
is another person who has different needs and values than we do,

and who holds a perspective of life that differs from our own. A clear example of an ownership perspective is slavery, or the practice of selling a woman for a dowry. In these situations, human beings become the property of another, and as property, they are expected to fulfill their owners' wishes.

If we hold the expectation that our bodies are obligated to make our lives convenient, and we make life plans without consulting our bodies' desires, that's an ownership. If we believe we have the right to impose our cultural values on our bodies without our bodies' consent, that's an ownership. If we believe we have the right to force our bodies to act, look, and behave in a way that is fundamentally antagonistic to who our bodies truly are, that's an ownership.

The upside of an ownership is that we get to control someone. We can manipulate them, harm them, degrade them, shame them, and physically force them to make them do what we want. We justify this by deciding that they are not as important as we are. In some way, we reason, they are less intelligent, less alive, less worthy, less human. We've employed this technique to claim ownership of our environment, plundering Mother Nature because we believe we own her. White Westerners have a long lineage of using this reasoning to massacre, enslave, sequester, and brutalize other races.

Ownership gives us control at the price of perpetual disconnection and constant vigilance. We get to control our bodies' emotions, size, shape, hunger, fatigue, and intuition. We get what we want without considering the perspective of the other being. But when we control someone, we can never be connected to them in a way that feeds our soul. We must always be on guard because we've created a battle between ourselves and the person we are controlling. When we're in an ownership with our bodies, we inevitably feel at war with them. And when we fight our bodies, we are destined to lose because we're ultimately fighting the intelligence of nature.

This begs the question: If body ownership gets you what you want, but you're not happy with what you get, is it really what you want?

What you really want is love. Ownership will get you everything but love.

OUR ANIMAL INSTINCTS

In undisturbed natural habitats, wild animals experience no chronic disease or obesity. By eating what they were made to eat and living how they were made to live, they effortlessly honor the symbiotic interactions with neighboring species and their environment. But when these same animals are put in zoos, they become diseased, infertile, apathetic, violent, and depressed. The zoo walls effectively prevent animals from expressing their instinctual wisdom. They often cannot eat the foods of their natural ecosystem, move across the terrain, or interact with other species with whom they've formed ancient, mutual relationships. After all, humans can never re-create a natural environment in a fenced enclosure.

If you don't know you're a slave, if you don't know
if you're isolated or oppressed, how do you fight to be free?

—YEONMI PARK

An animal's body is always informing her choices. She knows when to rest and for how long. She knows what to eat and how much. She knows when to mate, how to give birth, and raise healthy offspring without medical intervention. She's able to do this because she is fully connected to her natural environment and connected to her instinctual drives. In a zoo, however, she cannot exercise her inner wisdom because her environment prevents that. As a result, countless interventions are used to "rehabilitate" her into nonhabitual circumstances. She is given medications to treat diseases that never impact her wild cousins. As her weight spirals out of control, she receives special diets to make her lose or gain weight. When she is infertile, she undergoes fertility treatments.

Does this sound similar to the human condition? We've also put our own bodies in a zoo, and so face chronic rates of disease, infertility, apathy, violence, and depression. And it's for one simple reason: we are forcing our bodies into an environment where they cannot express their wisdom. Our bodies aren't stupid; we're simply preventing the expression of their infinite intelligence. The invisible corset separates us from the only wisdom that can save us.

OUR PARTNERSHIP LEGACY

The point is not for women simply to take power out of men's hands, since that wouldn't change anything about the world. It's a question precisely of destroying that notion of power.

—SIMONE DE BEAUVOIR

In the beginning, God was a woman. Paleolithic cave paintings and artifacts, dating back twenty thousand years, show evidence of Goddess worship and Goddess-oriented ritual. Whether painted, carved, or sculpted, the first God images were female. Venus figurines found across Europe from this time period attest to the widespread perception of the female body as sacred. And in all corners of the world, the oldest creation myths hold that the world was created from the Goddess's own body.

For a period of time, these Goddess-centered societies flourished with the shift from a hunting-gathering to an agrarian lifestyle. Farming allowed a reliable source of food and freed up time for women to creatively expand their culture. Women were the first potters, weavers, textile dyers, hide tanners, and plant medicine makers. In their book *The Great Cosmic Mother*, a landmark exploration of indigenous wisdom, authors Monica Sjöö and Barbara Mor write, "These tens of thousands of years of human culture were shaped and sustained by communities of creative, sexually and psychically active women—women who were inventors, producers, scientists, physicians, lawgivers, visionary shamans, artists."

These Goddess-oriented cultures were likely matrifocal and matrilineal, but not matriarchies. While women held preeminent cultural positions, and family lineage was traced through mothers, women did not dominate or subjugate men. These cultures show no evidence of distinct social hierarchy, inequality, or oppression of any group of people.

These cultures may have been the most peaceful human communities Earth has ever known. In her pivotal book *The Chalice and the Blade*, Riane Eisler examines the lifestyles and value systems of these Goddess-centered cultures. She points out that Neolithic art, in contrast to later art, lacks imagery of weapons, violence, and cruelty. Large caches of weapons and military fortifications are also absent from archaeological sites from this time. In their book, Sjöö and Mor explain, "Evidence shows that the farther back we go in human history, the gentler our species was. This is because the early matrifocal groups were concentrated on maintaining, rather than exploiting, life."

Then, nomadic invaders introduced a power shift that changed the course of human history. About seven thousand years ago, we see evidence of the disruption of peaceful Near Eastern cultures due to both invasions and natural catastrophes. Significant periods of invasion followed, targeting these and European agrarian communities. These invaders included Kurgans, Aryans, and early Semites such as the Levite tribe in the Old Testament. These groups held a completely radical perspective of community, one based on male dominance, violence, and hierarchy. Instead of valuing a nurturing Goddess, they worshipped a vengeful, warring God and created religious rules denigrating women as slaves, prostitutes, and property.

As these invaders conquered more and more territory, their value system became the norm in Europe. Previously, Westerners had perceived power as the ability to create and nurture life. Eisler describes this as a *partnership model* of social organization. Now, however, power was in the hands of those who could most effectively force, dominate, and kill. Eisler calls this the *dominator model*, which I'll refer to as domination power. Over the following centuries, this new domination power would be so thoroughly assimilated into Westerners' psyches and lifestyles that *we would assume it to be human nature rather than the loss of our true nature.*

Domination power informed every social structure and institution arising from Europe. Western science, religion, and education all rest on the foundation of the hierarchy imposed through force and cruelty. Colonization, the epitome of dominator power, spread across the globe into indigenous cultures that, like ancient Western Goddess-based cultures, knew only the partnership way of living.

As domination power shaped Western society, it also shaped our relationship to our bodies. As within, so without: we applied the same paradigm of hierarchy, force, and violence to our bodies. We cinch ourselves into the invisible corset, tightening the domination string as much as possible. We believe that the only way to exist in our bodies is to dominate them into submission so they conform with cultural beauty and productivity ideals. In the end, we're severing ourselves from our bodies' intuitive, emotional, and healing wisdom.

If this doesn't sound like anything you've read in history books, that's because much of ancient history is largely unknown, ignored, and erased. Knowledge is power, and history has been written by those who wish to hold power. If women don't know the lineage from which we came, we cannot return to it. Although our true history may not be taught in school, buried deep within our collective female psychic memory is the record of our true lineage: a time when women knew our power and the earth knew peace, a time to which we can return.

ISN'T BEAUTY BIOLOGICAL?

Over the last two years, I transitioned my social media platform from focusing on health to discussing body image and beauty culture.

While the majority of my community welcomed this direction, I came to expect variations of one comment every time I posted. "But isn't beauty a function of biology? Women are evolutionarily wired to compete for male attention through beauty, because beauty equals health and fertility. So it's women's nature to strive for beauty, and it's men's nature to prioritize beautiful women."

What is now called the nature of women is an artificial thing—the result of forced repression in some directions, unnatural stimulation in others.

—JOHN STEWART MILL

To create equality and safety for women, and a reality check for men, we have to call beauty culture what it is: a hierarchy that provides unearned privileges to some and denies equality to others. Like those afforded to white people in a racist society, these privileges are not based on the merit of the individual but are a result of social systems designed to unfairly consolidate power. In her book *The Beauty Bias*, Stanford professor Deborah Rhode dives into the data surrounding beauty discrimination.

According to Rhode, this discrimination manifests at an early age.

- Less attractive children receive less attention from teachers and parents than their more attractive counterparts, and they are less likely to be seen as good, smart, cheerful, likable, and socially skilled.

- Children, internalizing this prejudice, perceive attractive people as having better personality traits and desire them as friends.

- Girls, by the age of twelve, place more importance on their appearance than their competence.

This bias carries into the workplace.

* Employers are more likely to judge overweight individuals as less disciplined and socially skilled.

* When accompanied by a photograph of less attractive authors, written materials get lower ratings for style and creativity.

* Attractive faculty are more likely to receive positive feedback from students.

Rhode adds, "Not only are the less attractive treated worse, their unfavorable treatment can erode self-esteem, self-confidence, and social skills, which compound their disadvantages." Beauty bias creates toxic repercussions for society as a whole. In her TED Talk, Megan Ramsey reports that teenagers with less body confidence engage in less physical activity, eat fewer fruits and vegetables, have lower self-esteem, and are at greater risk of depression. Low body confidence impacts our careers, too, as 17 percent of women reported they would miss a job interview on a day they didn't feel confident about how they looked.

Ramsey asks, "Ever think about what this is doing to our economy? And if we could overcome this, what that opportunity looks like? Unlocking this potential is in the interest of every single one of us." When our culture perceives those who are conventionally attractive as superior, we lose out on the social contribution of those we see as less attractive. We self-sabotage as a community when we accept the premise that a biologically predestined hierarchy grants beautiful people more social acceptance and privileges.

There exist some culturally consistent beauty characteristics that correspond to health. This fact provides some credence to the theory that humans look for beauty in a mate in order to have genetically viable offspring. By and large, however, the biology argument is an ethically corrupt, logically unfeasible myth that perpetuates cruelty and inequality. It is both a product and tool of domination power, used to validate discrimination and the vast financial inequity that women shoulder in beauty culture. If we are to make social progress and uphold a basic level of morality, this hierarchical belief must go.

Why It's Not Biology

The biology argument consistently excuses inequality.

In 1869, John Stewart Mill published *The Subjection of Women*, a groundbreaking treatise that called the then-present state of marriage what it truly was: forced slavery of women. At the time of his writing, it was considered women's nature to be subservient to men. Mill countered by saying, "What is now called the nature of women is an eminently artificial thing—the result of forced repression in some directions, unnatural stimulation in others."

The "it's natural" argument has been employed to justify every system of oppression, from slavery to racism to sexism to homophobia. It's a cruel argument to leave unquestioned for it always benefits the oppressor. Mill summed this pattern up perfectly when he said, "Unnatural generally means only uncustomary, and that everything which is usual appears natural." He adds, "Was there ever any domination which did not appear natural to those who possessed it?"

Ever since Mary Wollstonecraft wrote the first feminist manifesto in 1790, it seems that every feminist in history has had to contend with the argument that the oppressive, restrictive expectations placed on us are biological. Wollstonecraft railed against Rousseau for suggesting it was women's nature to be meek, acquiescent, and predisposed to frilly dresses. Women striving for education in the 1800s protested the idea that education was beyond a woman's natural capacities. The suffragettes faced objections that voting would impede a woman's natural obligation to care for home, husband, and family. Dissenters to second-wave feminism in the 1960s believed a woman's natural place was in the home, not the workforce. Now, we are being told that it's only natural we spend so much time, money, and suffering trying to appeal to a beauty standard.

In her book *All The Rage*, Darcy Lockman explores the data that runs contrary to the popular assumption that human nature explains the unequal division of childcare in modern partnerships. Even when both parents work full time, women still carry the brunt of childcare and housework—about 65 percent of it. We may assume biology explains why the majority of childrearing falls to women, but data suggests this is not instinctual but societal. Social progress demands we stop using the myth of biology to perpetuate this inequality. Lockman quotes neuroscientist and author Lise Eliot:

> *Calling gendered division of labor "innate" is a convenient way of maintaining the power structure, period. . . . Everything you call a sex difference, if you take a different perspective—what's the power angle on this—often explains things. It has served men very well to assume that male-female differences are hardwired. It's been harmful for women to live that. (Emphasis mine.)*

Whenever we find the biology argument justifying inequality, exploitation, or harm of other beings, the first question we must ask is, "How does this argument serve the current hierarchy of power?"

The beauty standard varies drastically based on cultural and time influences.

There are a few features we consider beautiful—such as facial symmetry and clear skin—that span culture and time, and this suggests an evolutionary influence. Research indicates that many indigenous cultures consider a low waist-hip-ratio—meaning a smaller waist with larger hips or posterior—a sign of attractiveness. Although data remains questionable, it suggests this body type may correlate to better fertility for women. If we are at the mercy of our evolutionary drives, it would make sense that men would prioritize these features in a mate for childbearing.

That doesn't mean, however, that the subconscious mechanisms at play in biological mate selection are fooled by the instruments and interventions of beauty culture. As I discussed, Botox freezes the subtle muscles around the eyes, which may impede the subconscious messages of safety between people. On a biological level, it's likely that fillers don't make someone look more fertile—just more artificial. In the same way, we can't assume that a waist trainer or fat injections into the buttocks make a woman appear more fertile because it was achieved through artificial means rather than healthy genetics. The subconscious, intuitive perception of a potential mate might know the difference. By and large, we internalize attractiveness due to nurture, *not* nature.

It's due to cultural conditioning, for example, that someone might find a face more attractive when it's layered with foundation, concealer, highlighter, bronzer, eyeshadow, eyebrow powder, mascara, and lipstick. These beauty trends vary significantly throughout cultures and history. In ancient Egypt, both women and men applied brightly colored mineral pigments around their eyes. In Elizabethan times, women plucked their hairline and eyebrows, but now we value bold brows. In Marie Antoinette's royal court, women powered their face a stark white, but recent trends lead women to tan their fair skin.

Plumpness also goes in and out of fashion. Art from the 1600s through the 1800s shows an emphasis on curves, featuring women with full bellies, breasts, and hips. Then, in the late 1800s, an artificially narrowed waist came into style with corsetry, followed by the flapper aesthetic of the 1920s. In the following decades, the idealized female body would expand into the curvaceous icons of the 1950s and shrink to the skeletal "heroin chic" models on 1990s runways. Food availability may also determine weight preference. There's a correlation between thinness being prized in cultures where food is easily accessible, while fatness is beautiful in cultures where food is scarce.

Further, the mere-exposure effect suggests that familiarity influences what we find most attractive. Coined by Robert Zajonc, this concept arose from his work when he presented study participants with different images. Initially, the visual stimuli included foreign words, Chinese characters, and pictures of strangers' faces. The more the participants saw and became familiar with each image, the more they claimed they liked it.

Consider the number of ads we see daily, on TV, social media, and in print. Given this volume, we interact with "media bodies" more frequently than "real-life bodies." Now think about the representation of racial diversity, facial features, and body types. Sure, there may be a little more variety than we saw thirty years ago, but the images we are exposed to lean heavily toward the white, heteronormative, and makeup-laden. Because media images actively condition our definition of beautiful, and that definition of beautiful feeds into beauty bias and racism, the research on repeated exposure raises an ethical question.

Additionally, culture heavily influences sexual fetishes and sexual attractiveness, so often assumed to be biological. For example, in the early 1800s, when it was considered improper for a woman to show any portion of her leg in public, men commonly had ankle fetishes. Presently, our obsession with breasts, like earlier ankle fetishes, arose in response to Western culture scandalizing and commercializing this part of a woman's body. In the majority of US states, it's illegal for a woman to go topless, yet one can stream porn instantly or purchase *Playboy* magazines at any corner store. This industry domination of the female body is intended to create profits, not to promote cultural morality. Even labia now have a beauty standard, fueling the rates of surgical alteration of the vulva (labiaplasty). This is because we're not exposed to the normal spectrum of vulvas but only a sliver of homogenous-looking genitalia on porn.

Beauty culture is racist, and racism is not biological.

Evolutionary forces do not drive us to destroy genetic diversity in favor of Eurocentric homogeneity. Yet this is the theme of beauty culture, particularly in cosmetic surgery. It gained a foothold in America with rhinoplasty, Rhode explains in *The Beauty Bias,* when a significant number of Jews wanted less distinctive noses. To this day, people get nose jobs to straighten or narrow their noses, making them appear not biologically more beautiful but to typify Anglo features. In Asia, for example, rhinoplasty commonly includes adding height to the nose to make the profile resemble a "typical" Western nose. Similarly, eyelid surgery is common in Asia to create a double eyelid—erasing a hereditary feature in favor of a Western beauty ideal.

Beauty culture puts inordinately more pressure on women, rather than men, to change their bodies. In the same way, it puts drastically more pressure on people of color, rather than white people, to change their bodies. Just as the invisible corset is held in place by invisible threads, so is racism. In fact, beauty culture is one of the unseen strings that hold systemic racism in place.

Consider also the discrimination black people face for wearing natural or traditional black hairstyles in offices, schools, and sports. Black students have received detention, been banned from prom, or been required to change their hair to participate in sporting events. Black women in jobs ranging from news anchors to store employees have been told their hair is "unprofessional," "too black," or "inappropriate." In 2017, California became the first state to ban hair discrimination. Of course, hair discrimination is not about professionalism. In this situation, professionalism plays the same function as the female gender role—it's a social construct designed to control and oppress a group of people by first shaping how we perceive that group.

Racist values also feed into our culture's thinness obsession. Prior to the late 1800s, plumpness indicated prosperity for men, and women's full hips were idealized, even emphasized with bustles. Then, as the agricultural economy in America took off in the late 1800s, and plenty of food was available to most Americans, plumpness no longer indicated a higher social status. Now, upper-class Americans sought another way to uphold visual differentiation of the social hierarchy. In her book *Losing It: False Hopes and Fat Profits in the Diet Industry*, Laura Fraser writes, "Well-to-do Americans of northern European extraction wanted to be able to distinguish themselves, physically and racially, from stockier immigrants." Thinness, like whiteness, provided a visible distinction of the "us vs. them" racist belief system. Thinness was never truly about beauty, but social control and hierarchy.

Large lips and butts, stereotypical feature of African bodies, were once widely shamed in Western culture. In the early 1800s, caricatures depicted African Americans with overemphasized lips, and compared their facial features to apes. Now, lip injections are one of the most popular surgeries in the United States. This is not biological, it glorifies a feature we condemned only a few generations ago. It's cultural appropriation, which occurs when we commercialize the body features, beliefs, or rituals we once condemned in an oppressed group of people. Black feminist scholar bell hooks explains, "Within commodity culture, ethnicity becomes spice, seasoning that can liven up the dull dish that is mainstream white culture." If the beauty standard, and the accompanying beauty bias in the school and workplace, creates pressure and incentive to erase our biological heritage from our bodies, it is not a matter of beauty. It's a matter of racism and civil rights.

The men aren't doing it.

If sexual attractiveness creates the biological imperative behind women's body modification, why aren't men compelled toward the same behaviors? Why, for example, aren't men undergoing testes implants to lift aging, sagging balls, just like women are getting breast implants? If the appearance of fertility is a driving force, then men, whose virility declines with age, would have a similar imperative to fake youth with invasive procedures. "Oh, but that would look so unnatural, testes aren't supposed to be symmetrical. Plus, testicle size doesn't matter to a man's sexual performance," one might think. Yet our culture seems to believe those myths when it comes to breasts.

"But not *all men* escape the pressure to alter their bodies and conform to a beauty standard," one might also counter. That's true, and it must not distract from the fact that beauty culture is a sexist system that primarily harms women's bodies and women's socioeconomic status.

For example, women made up 94 percent of the total Botox procedures in 2018. Men also seek hair loss treatments and hair transplants, and in 2017, the US hair transplant industry was valued at $1.7 billion. Compare this with the US beauty industry valued at $88 billion that same year. Further, it doesn't help the men who are struggling with body dysmorphia to excuse beauty culture with statements such as, "It's just the way things are. You have to change your body before you feel confident. Just look at the women, after all!"

In her hilarious feminist memoir, *How to Be a Woman*, Caitlin Moran illustrates the cosmetic surgery pressure on the women attending an awards ceremony for England's celebrity elite. Moran writes:

> *The men's faces are just as you would expect— famous and nonfamous alike, the men just look like, well, men. . . . But the women: oh, the women all look the same. . . . In the same way that you can tell if some sexism is happening to you by asking the question, "Is this polite, or not?" you can tell whether some misogynistic societal pressure is being exerted on women by calmly enquiring, "And are the* men *doing this, as well?"*

Then she explains the conclusion that one might draw: "If they aren't, chances are you're dealing with what we strident feminists refer to as 'some total fucking bullshit.'"

We are not simply at the mercy of our biological drives.

The biology argument attempts to explain how, in our society, conventionally beautiful people reap benefits at the expense of less attractive people, even though we have a brain capable of making ethical decisions. It also provides an excuse for some men to cling to a God complex by confusing their culturally indoctrinated judgments with evolutionary programing. Men entrenched in beauty culture tend to seek external validation by being partnered with, or desired by, beautiful women. They obtain a sense of superiority by criticizing or complimenting a woman's appearance, often assuming their judgments about women's appearances actually matter in some grand evolutionary scheme of things.

If we look elsewhere in society, however, we find ourselves wholly capable of overriding our best fertility and genetic interests. What of putting hormone-disrupting chemicals in our personal care products? What of poisoning our livestock with hormones and antibiotics, that then disrupt our own microbiome? What about working while sitting for eight hours per day, which is correlated to higher rates of chronic disease? What about surrounding ourselves with blue light emitted from electronic devices, which disrupts our sleep and hormone balance? What about the electromagnetic frequencies from our devices, which are linked to developmental disorders, cancer, and infertility?

Fertility rates are at an all-time low, while diseases of civilization such as asthma, allergies, cancer, and chronic illness skyrocket. If we are not able to outmaneuver the genetic drive to produce the healthiest offspring, how do we explain this brazen self-destruction? We ignore the biological imperatives for our health and the health of our environment. Surely, we can override whatever slight biological programming might influence the inequities of beauty culture.

If beauty is biological, we shouldn't have to be intimidated or shamed into it.

If it were truly in women's best evolutionary interest to adhere to the present beauty standard, then, according to the biology argument and given free will, we would choose to do so. The beauty industry wouldn't need to employ coercive, body-shaming, and fear-based techniques to sell billions of dollars of products.

Our beauty behavior stems from cultural training, not instinct. Imagine if you weren't taught to hate your body. Would you be buying so many products to "fix" yourself? Would you still try to hide your cellulite or belly from your lover, or would you feel more sexually emboldened? Would you enjoy more trust and less guilt around food? Would you spend less on beauty products and more on soul-expanding experiences like travel and education? If women were naturally inclined to spend so much money and incur so much pain to change our bodies, then there would be no need for shaming marketing techniques. The fact that beauty advertisers employ so much fear-based social indoctrination reveals why our obsession with beauty *isn't* biological.

WHAT BODY PARTNERSHIP FEELS LIKE

Imagine a hectic Saturday, when the items on your to-do list can't fit onto a single piece of paper. In addition to the laundry, errands, and grocery shopping, your boss has insisted you complete a project before Monday morning. At 1 p.m., you're in the middle of talking to a colleague on the phone, finalizing details on the project, and tension has inched your shoulders up to your ears. Having missed lunch, you swallow half-chewed bites of a protein bar while you speak. In the midst of your cell phone conversation, you hear a firm knock on your door.

Nothing can bring you peace but yourself.
—RALPH WALDO EMERSON

The last thing you need is an interruption, but the knocking persists. You open the door, cell phone still pressed against your ear. You look into the face of a woman who looks just like you, except she's well rested and radiating a queenlike calmness. She reminds you of Mary Poppins.

As you realize your mouth is gaping, she steps across the threshold and takes the cell phone out of your hand.

"No, wait. I'm talking on that," you say. The sparkling version of yourself now holds the phone to her own mouth and says, with a voice that sounds exactly like your own, except clear and calm, "I just realized I'm not able to have this conversation now. I really value having this project finalized and working with you in a collaborative, effective manner. I can't do that until I take a break to care for myself, so I'll call you back in an hour."

"Why did you do that?" you say. "I don't have time for a break!"

This magical twin-like stranger says, "Sit down at the table." She speaks gently, but holds you with a firm gaze. You glance back at your cell phone but something inside you says, *Resistance is futile.* She takes away the remains of the chalky protein bar and says, "This is not a meal."

She opens your fridge and rummages about. She pulls out eggs, some bell peppers, spinach, and butter. You watch as she deftly makes an omelet and places it in front of you. "This is exactly what you want to eat," she says. And it is. You take one bite, and as soon as you swallow, you feel a soothing warmth throughout your body.

"You're going to take a twenty minute nap," the woman says. "Then you're going to do laundry without doing anything else. *Then* you're going to call your colleague, and you'll know exactly how to proceed with the project. You'll finish it quickly, and then you'll call your boyfriend and ask him to pick up dinner. You don't need to cook tonight. Enjoy a relaxing evening."

Fifteen minutes earlier, you didn't have enough time to breathe. Now, you can't help but believe this woman who told you to rest, and then promised a calm evening when the entirety of your life felt urgently incomplete.

"Before I rest, can you tell me something?" you ask. "I've been fighting with my boyfriend recently, and I don't know if this relationship is right for me. He seems distant, and I don't know what's up. Also, I don't even know if my job is right for me! I think I secretly hate it, but I can't imagine how I could change jobs."

"Oh, honey," she says, "I know exactly what you should do. I can't tell you how it's going to turn out because that's not how I guide you. But I can always tell you what do to, one step at a time. All you have to do is ask me for the next step."

After finishing the omelet, you walk to your bedroom in a slight daze and slip under the covers for the prescribed nap. While you don't understand what is happening, you feel a bone-deep sense of peace. You know when you wake up from your nap, you'll have the next answer you need. You don't need to understand those answers, just like you don't need to understand why this luminous version of yourself hung up on a critical phone call and made you a plate of eggs. All you know is hanging up, and eating, and resting *worked*. You feel better. Left to your own devices, you would never grant yourself the permission to do these things. But you surrender to her wisdom because you know she is the one who will lead you to a magnificent life.

LETTING THE LOVE IN

Cutting the strings of body hatred does not mean learning to love your body. Love requires no instruction; it comes as naturally and as easily as breathing. We must simply unlearn the ways we've blocked love and self-love from our lives. As stated in the spiritual text *A Course in Miracles*, "Your task is not to seek for love, but merely to seek and find all the barriers within yourself that you have built against it."

When we're dominating our bodies, we can't let the love in. We can't let our bodies take care of us. We refuse to rest, play, relax, and experience joy in our bodies because we are so busy trying to control them. Love is, inherently, a loss of control. It's a conscious dissolving of the walls we've built to protect ourselves from pain. If we keep the pain out, we also keep the healing out. Sometimes, love hurts. But it is also the only thing that heals.

Do you want to dominate your body, or do you want to be cared for by her?

Do you want to control your body, or do you want to be connected to her?

Do you want to own your body, or do you want to know love?

CHAPTER FOUR

DISCONNECTION

To be native to a place we must learn to speak its language.

—ROBIN KIMMERER

The first time I heard a flower speak to me, I was traipsing through a Hawaiian jungle. It was as if a little purple bloom raised its hand and said, "Pick me!" The words rushed joyfully through my body, and I knew she was offering herself in service to my wellbeing. What I didn't know at the time was that in ancient cultures, shamans and tribal healers formulated their plant medicines because the flowers sang to them about the healing they could offer humanity.

Later, I found a TED Talk by Dr. Wade Davis, an expert on psychedelic plants, who discussed anthropological research on plants speaking to humans. He described how indigenous peoples created ayahuasca, a plant medicine used in sacred rituals. The hallucinogenic properties of ayahuasca arise when two different parts of two different plants are combined into the plant medicine. Given the tens of thousands of plants in the region where it is made, including many varieties that look indistinguishable, there's no way the ayahuasca recipe could be created through trial and error. One Amazonian culture had over seventeen different varieties of ayahuasca, identifiable because the subspecies of one plant, the native people said, sang in different keys on the night of a full moon.

Sometimes, when I'm in nature and relaxed in the present moment, I'll hear the flower songs. It's not a tune I could hum; it's like silent music filling my body. Walking up to a flowering bush, I might feel my heart bursting, as if to the ecstatic swell of violins. With other flowers, I might feel a sensual lusciousness, like golden honey flowing through my body. I often see clear mental images or hear words from the plants telling me of the healing properties they have to share. I'll feel profound emotional shifts in the plant's presence. Have you ever been so moved by a piece of music that the beauty of it is breathtaking and unbearable and rapturous all at once? To me, that's what the flower songs feel like.

As I tried to make sense of my experience, I didn't find much help from scientific literature. Turns out, there are no studies on plant songs. Anthropological research, however, led me down a rabbit hole of information not just related to plants. I learned that some individuals in indigenous tribes see silver lines of light on the horizon when they are tracking an animal. These lines are connected to animals' spirits and reveal the path an animal took. Some people have an innate gift for tracking—they are immediately connected with the energy of an animal, as well as visual impressions of it, by touching its footprint on the ground. Certain African tribes once relied on telepathic communication between individuals at the home base and those on hunting expeditions. In many indigenous communities, certain individuals communicated with underground water sources, sensing the presence of water through the phenomenon of dowsing. And across the globe, ancient cultures intuited their nutritional needs so well that they had negligible rates of chronic illness, infertility, and birth defects.

After a while, I stopped asking, "How weird is it that these cultures thought humans could communicate with nature?" and started asking, "What's so weird about Western culture that we think we *can't* communicate with nature?" Our skepticism results from being disconnected from the wisdom of nature within our bodies; this in turn separates us from the wisdom of nature outside of us.

Disconnection from our bodies' wisdom is the third corset string. The chronic body hatred we face is a disease of disconnection. In *The Great Cosmic Mother*, Monica Sjöö and Barbara Mor write:

> *Modern sickness is that of disconnection, the ego unable to feel an organic part of the world . . . But when the healers—the physicians of mind and body—do not know themselves what it is we need to be connected to, how can they solve the syndrome of disconnection?*

We need to reconnect to our bodies.

WHY WE'RE DISCONNECTED

At age eleven, I was anorexic, bitter, angry, and resentful. Loneliness pierced my heart like an arrow. I didn't know what to do with all these emotions because those feelings seemingly weren't allowed in my house, my religious community, or my school environment. So I withdrew from life. My parents took me to the doctor, who gave me a pill to stop me from feeling so much. This pill didn't make my life better because I remained in the same feeling-phobic environment, imprisoned by my self-imposed silence. The pill made me feel farther away from my body, and farther away from my life.

Relationships with our bodies are social,
political, and economic inheritances.

—SONYA RENEE TAYLOR

The belief that what I *looked* like mattered more than what I *felt* like also took root at that age. The fitness industry told me that my body was for *shaping*. I began each day running on the treadmill, followed by ten minutes of ab work. It felt obligatory and boring. Movement no longer connected me to self-expression or joy, as when I was younger, doing gymnastics or playing soccer. Now it was penance and punishment for eating. I also disconnected from my hunger. If my stomach still felt empty after a breakfast of oatmeal with Splenda and seven almonds, I tried to escape the sensation by chewing gum, drinking Diet Coke, or recalculating my lunchtime caloric allotment.

I look back at the series of events that led me to disconnect from my body at such a vulnerable age. There was the medical perspective that examined symptoms rather than environments, and the doctor who prescribed the antidepressant. There was also the chain of individuals who taught me it was necessary to strive for the "perfect" body. There were the models who whittled themselves down to skeletons on 900 calories a day, and the fashion houses who put these models on fashion runways. There was the magazine editor who ran articles championing extreme weight-loss diets, and articles telling me I should fear having a rounded tummy or untoned upper arms. There was the photo editor who narrowed the waist of the cover celebrity, and the celebrity herself who spent hundreds of thousands of dollars on making her body become a beauty standard impossible to achieve without that much money.

Did any of these people intend to disconnect me from my body? No. But, knowingly or unknowingly, they were part of a system that exploits well-meaning, naïve individuals to escalate the rate of body divorce. Body disconnection is not an accident because it counteracts the intrinsic drive toward health that's embedded in every manifestation of nature, including the human body. This disconnection is the intention of industries that seek to control us so that they may gain profits and power, for we must first be distanced from our intuition to be controlled.

The pharmaceutical *industry* wants you disconnected from your emotions because that's how they sell medications to mask symptoms rather than addressing root problems. The diet *industry* wants you disconnected from your sense of hunger and intuitive cues around food, so you'll spend money every year on the supplements, gadgets, and books for a new fad diet. The fashion *industry* wants you disconnected from your body's comfortable weight so you'll buy more clothes as your body size fluctuates with yo-yo dieting.

We need body-connected change makers to infiltrate and recon-struct these industries. We need:

- politicians who say, "No, I will not take funding from Big Pharma or diet product lobbyists."

- doctors who say, "No, I will not prescribe medications without also providing education and resources for body reconnection."

- models who say, "No, I will not starve myself to perpetuate a toxic body standard."

- clothing designers who say, "No, I will not hire models who engage in disordered eating."

- magazine editors who say, "No, I will not publish articles or advertisements that glorify dieting and anti-aging."

- celebrities who say, "No, I will not have my body photoshopped or surgically altered."

Many of these change makers are here, but we need more.

How Body Disconnection Manifests Itself

There are three primary ways that body disconnection manifests itself.

Prioritizing your appearance over your experience.

Beauty messages tell us that the state of our outsides are more important than our insides, that our internal experience of physical and mental health pales in comparison to the importance of our appearance. This is summed up by what Kate Moss said in the late 2000s—and is still used for "fitspiration"—"Nothing tastes as good as skinny feels." Do you know what skinny feels like, when you're restricting food groups, counting calories, and spending an inordinate amount of time at the gym, doing exercises you hate? It feels like deprivation, self-hatred, 24/7 food obsession, and an all-consuming anxiety that the waiter forgot you requested "dressing on the side" for your salad. It does not feel good.

I tell my clients: "Nothing looks as good as mental health feels." After I help them get off the yo-yo diet roller coaster and teach them intuitive eating, my clients start feeling tremendously more calm. Maybe they're not as thin as they were that one time they managed to cut out carbs for a month, but they're healthier now that they relish the pleasure of food, eat mindfully, move joyfully, and are thinking about things besides calories consumed and calories burned. They've also improved their quality of life by feeling more sensual, relaxed, and connected to those around them.

Valuing outer appearance over inner experience also commonly manifests with our clothing choices. I consider how I started wearing padded bras when I was a flat-chested fourteen-year-old, anxious to convince others that my body was maturing more quickly than it actually was. I wore those bras in an attempt to ameliorate my body shame, but they only compounded the problem. I felt paranoid that someone would brush up against me and notice the artificial firmness of the cups, revealing my body as a fraud. Those underwire bras also produced a pervasive discomfort, but I believed I needed them to be womanly enough—just as our great-grandmothers believed of their corsets.

I eventually gave up on padded bras, but then I found myself in a relationship with a man who wanted me to wear lingerie. I naïvely believed, as he did, that he was entitled to my body matching his aesthetic preferences. So I bought lingerie even though it itched, poked, rode up, and made me hate myself for spending money on something that I tore off the minute I was at home alone. If I could go back, I'd tell my old self, "Honey, you don't *ever* have to wear uncomfortable underwear—*ever*. Feeling comfortable in your body is always sexier than feeling like you're wearing spiderwebs made out of barbed wire and steel wool." (I have heard that some women truly like wearing lingerie. For me, that is hard to believe. But I truly like hot yoga and have been told by other women that's hard to believe, so to each her own.)

The physical discomfort caused by certain clothing, specific grooming practices, and dieting creates a constant distraction. We have to exert

additional mental and psychic energy to override that distraction—
especially those of us who are highly sensitive—and we normalize this
invisible mental labor. Consider how many types of women's clothing
are inherently uncomfortable, just like corsets were: skyscraper heels,
control-top undergarments, skin-tight dresses, many varieties of bras.
These clothing items tell us that the default experience of being a
woman is discomfort and pain.

EXERCISE: Practice Reconnection

Notice when you make choices about your appearance, and
start asking yourself, "What would make me more physically
comfortable?"

If you're blow-drying your hair, and your arms are aching, and
you're stressed about being late for work, you might ask, "Would
having short hair make me more physically comfortable?"

If you're wincing as hot wax is applied to your labia, you might
ask, "Would a patch of pubic hair be more physically comfortable?"

If you're longing to jump in the pool, but you're concerned about
your mascara running, you might ask, "Would skipping makeup on
superhot days make me more physically comfortable?"

Withholding body acceptance.

When clients come to me, they often believe that self-acceptance is a
reward to earn once they get thin enough, healthy enough, or successful
enough. "I can't accept my body as it is," they express in different ways.
"If I accept myself, it's like giving myself a pass to be unhealthy and
unmotivated." I find the same response online, when I educate about
the importance of accepting your body no matter how heavy you are.

"It's dangerous for obese people to accept their bodies," commenters will say, ignoring the fact that one's weight is not always an indication of their personal health choices, nor is one's health status ever a reason to shame them.

The question is not, "Is it healthy to applaud one's unhealthy coping mechanisms?" but rather, "Is it healthy to accept one's body?" Acceptance carries the energy of love, the only energy capable of healing. When we shelve body acceptance as some reward we must earn, it ultimately and always backfires. That approach keeps us in the energy of fear, which always sabotages wholeness and wellbeing. To reconnect to our bodies, we must first accept them just as they are right now. For how can we ever reconnect to someone who we're ashamed of or afraid of?

Body rejection is the opposite of body acceptance, and it fuels the unhealthy coping mechanisms we're trying to escape. When a woman comes to me who is struggling with binge eating, for example, her eating issues always stem from some form of stress, trauma, hate, or dieting itself. She pours more fuel on the fire by hating how her body looks or behaves. Body rejection sends a message to our nervous system: "I am not safe with myself."

Let me explain this with a quick biology lesson. The nervous system operates in one of two states: sympathetic, also called fight-or-flight, and parasympathetic, or rest-and-digest. The state of our nervous system is not primarily determined by our external reality, but by our interpretation and perception of reality. If you perceive safety, your body relaxes into parasympathetic, and your body's biological healing processes can function optimally. You'll find it easy to relax, appreciate the present moment, and experience sensual pleasure. If you perceive danger, however, your nervous system prepares to fight, flee, or freeze. This puts a damper on repair processes in the body, reduces sleep quality, increases anxiety, and impairs digestion.

Body acceptance tells our nervous system, "I'm safe." Body rejection, on the other hand, says, "I'm not safe." Given that, what do you think better encourages healing and self-care? Once my clients start accepting their bodies, their stress reduces, and they have less need for the unhealthy habits they use to cope with stress. Telling anyone that they shouldn't accept their body isn't merely uninformed, it's unethical.

PRACTICE Reconnecting

Finish the sentence: "I'll accept my body . . ."

For example:

when I lose 20 pounds.

when I have fewer wrinkles.

when I reach orgasm faster.

Determine the emotional experience you want as a result of that. If numerous emotions come to mind, write them all down, and choose one that has the most charge or intensity. Then complete the thought with, "As a result I'll feel . . ."

Examples:

I'll accept my body when I lose twenty pounds. As a result I'll feel confident.

I'll accept my body when I have fewer wrinkles. As a result I'll feel relaxed.

I'll accept my body when I reach orgasm faster. As a result I'll feel sexual.

Now cross out the "when/as a result" statements:

I'll accept my body when I ~~lose 20 pounds. As a result I'll~~ feel confident.

I'll accept my body when I ~~have fewer wrinkles. As a result I'll~~ feel relaxed.

I'll accept my body when I ~~reach orgasm faster. As a result I'll~~ feel sexual.

Working with one statement at a time, start each morning asking yourself, "How can I have the experience of [desired emotion] today?" You might journal a few ideas to create that feeling in your day.

When we feel the need to change our appearance, it's not because that's the ultimate goal. We're using body modification and alteration as a means to a positive emotional experience. But the means are always the end. As long as we use the mindset of body rejection, that's the only outcome we'll ever experience—no matter how much our body changes.

When doing this exercise, please note that words like *beautiful* or *desirable* do not describe feelings because they are statements of someone else's perception of you. What we ultimately want is to *feel* good in our bodies, not to be judged positively by someone. Whenever we want someone's positive judgment of our bodies, it's because we think that's the way we're going to feel loved, safe, connected, expressive, or happy. Take the shortcut, and just go straight to creating that feeling in your life now.

Feelings are felt experiences in your body. Here are some examples:

Positive feelings: joyful, grateful, exhilarated, excited, aroused, peaceful, affectionate, inspired, hopeful, renewed, fulfilled, enchanted, delighted, calm, amazed, blissful

Negative feelings: hurt, sad, anxious, timid, angry, irritated, afraid, scared, confused, fatigued, tense, numb, helpless, uncomfortable, embarrassed, ashamed, exhausted, depleted, grief, appalled, shocked

Then there are pseudo-feelings—they're not real feelings, but reflect your judgment of someone's behavior or situation. Judgments are not feelings, they are mental ideas.

Pseudo-feelings include: abandoned, betrayed, invalidated, manipulated, misunderstood, disrespected, unseen, provoked, threatened, victimized, ignored.

Expecting consistency, not cycles, from our bodies.

My clients tell me all the time that something is wrong with them or their bodies because circumstances should be different. They say things like:

"I should lose the weight I gained after menopause started."

"I should achieve my pre-baby body."

"I should dye my gray hair."

"I should always have salads for lunch, even in the winter when I crave warm foods."

"I should have a stable weight throughout my menstrual cycle."

"I should have processed these emotions by now."

All these *shoulds* arise from comparison.

In turn, I ask my clients, "What standard are you comparing your body to, and is that standard valid and helpful? Or is that standard inhumane and causing body disconnection?" All the *should* statements result from the fallacy that the human body is supposed to remain the same throughout a day, month, year, or life cycle. Whenever we judge our bodies according to an unnatural standard, we inevitably reject and disconnect from them.

One of the primary ways we disconnect from our bodies is by comparing them to an unnatural standard of consistency rather than their intrinsic cycles. Nature is cyclical, and the force of nature outside of us works in the same manner within us. Our bodies go through cycles every day, year, and lifetime. When we honor those cycles, instead of coercing our bodies into machine-like consistency, we swim with the current of our lives rather than against it.

For example, before recognizing the value of cycles, I tried to make my menstrual cycle conform to my usual routine. When I experienced extreme fatigue the day before my period, I tried to push through with caffeine and willpower. When I got cramps the first day of my period, I popped painkillers and tried to plod through my usual to-do list. When my weight fluctuated throughout the month, I felt panicky and tried to fight my increased hunger before my period. I didn't realize it at the time, but I was fighting against my body by not honoring her cycles. I was also missing out on a profound opportunity for intuitive insight and restoration.

In her book *Awakening Intuition*, author Mona Lisa Schulz discusses how the right hemisphere of the brain receives intuitive information. When she is premenstrual (after ovulation), a woman's right hemisphere becomes more language oriented, and she notices more negative feeling words like *grief, sadness,* and *depression.* Schulz theorizes that our premenstrual brains are primed to focus on what's not working in our lives, thus indicating what we need to eliminate and release.

Now, I orient my work decisions around my menstrual cycle. First, I use an app called Natural Cycles to track my ovulation and period. When I feel extremely fatigued the day prior to my period, I give myself permission to spend the day gently. Similarly, the day my period starts, I feel extremely withdrawn and often struggle to make logical, analytical decisions. Instead of pushing through, I focus on intuitive insight, journaling, and self-reflection—all processes critical to my business and life choices.

PRACTICE Reconnection

Consider any *should* thoughts or statements you make about your body that conform to a societal standard or body fashion. For example:

> I should keep my weight stable throughout my life.
>
> I should get my lips enlarged.
>
> I should have visible abs.

Now change the sentence the following way:

> ~~I should~~ I don't have to keep my weight stable throughout my life before I like myself.
>
> ~~I should~~ I don't have to get my lips enlarged before I like myself.
>
> ~~I should~~ I don't have to have visible abs before I like myself.

Self-acceptance allows you to reconnect to your body even in the face of bullying external standards. Self-loathing and body shame, which masquerade under the guise of body "shoulds and shouldn'ts," halt you from tuning in to your body's wisdom.

You might be thinking, "But, Lauren, you don't understand! It's not heathy or safe for me to accept my body as it is right now!" No, that's not true. Please kindly see the earlier point about withholding body acceptance.

Comparing our bodies to other women's bodies.

A woman's magazine published an article comparing how men and women perceive the ideal woman's body. Women, apparently, desire Jennifer Aniston's uplifted breasts, but men want a woman to have Sofía Vergara's tremendous chest. Legs, hair, and butts were similarly assessed, as if this ideal mythical being were a human Build-A-Bear. This type of comparison absolutely epitomizes objectification. Instead of honoring the unique *reality* of our bodies, we fall into the fallacy that our bodies should conform to some fictional, alternative reality. The greatest spiritual teachers tell us that this rejection of *what is* creates perpetual suffering. "Realize deeply that the present moment is all you have," says Eckhart Tolle. Unless we find peace with our bodies *in the present moment*, we'll *never* find peace with our bodies.

Just like clothing, body types go in and out of fashion based on time and environment. I used to live in an area that neighbors Scottsdale, Arizona, a city with high rates of cosmetic surgery. Walking through a Scottsdale mall, I saw many women with lip injections and enlarged breasts. I contrast these women with the ballet bodies I envied as a young dancer, which could be described as emaciated A-cup athletes. I once thought they were the ultimate definition of beautiful, just like my friends, who used to do fitness competitions, once believed that ultimate beauty was silicone breasts perched above washboard abs, all a sun-kissed shade of extra-extra-dark spray tan.

Women in other places may set their sights on other body fads, like the Amazonian catwalk model or the dewy-skinned magazine-cover type. One of my mentors was a hair stylist and makeup artist in a prior life chapter. Once, she was doing makeup for a fashion show, and one of the models she was preparing was a Victoria's Secret model. My mentor said to the woman, "I could never look like you do in a bathing suit." The model replied, "I don't even look like that!" Because of tape, padding, contouring, and Photoshop, the beauty standard isn't realistic even for those who supposedly set that standard.

All these body types, against which women compare their own bodies, are fads. They go in and out of fashion just like pantsuits. Whereas fashion comes and goes with the decades and is dictated by someone else, style is unique, enduring, self-defined. It's time we let our bodies express their true style rather than force them to fit a fashionable fad. (You'll learn how to do this in chapter 9.)

Clients sometimes tell me, "I need to lose weight for my husband," or, "I'm contemplating getting breast implants because my boyfriend is a 'breast man.'" I choke down my immediate response, which is, "If your boyfriend likes breasts so much, tell *him* to get a boob job!" Like these clients, I once believed I needed my body to look a certain way to make other people like me. In my first relationship, my partner commented every time my weight fluctuated. I believed I needed to change my body to garner his approval. Only later did I realize that it's not loving when someone—a romantic partner, family member, or colleague—gives you conditional attention or respect based on your appearance.

If you are dating, sleeping with, or married to someone who has a problem with your body, the problem is not your body. I repeat: *the problem is not your body.* The problem, usually, is their perceptions limit their ability to love you. You don't need to change your body to be worthy of love, and most importantly, to be worthy of your own self-love. There is no normal body, no ideal body. Those are illusory concepts and as toxic as suggesting there's a superior race. There is your body and another woman's body, and it is disrespectful to everyone involved to compare the two. She is the yardstick for herself, and you are the yardstick for yourself.

PRACTICE Reconnection

Remembering the difference between true feelings and judgments identified in the previous exercise, consider an aspect of another woman's body that you've envied. Then fill in the rest of the following sentence: "I wish I had her _____ because I feel _____ about my own." For example:

> I wish I had her perky breasts because I feel embarrassed about my own.
>
> I wish I had her flat stomach because I feel uncomfortable about my own.
>
> I wish I had her clear skin because I feel ashamed about my own.

Now, rewrite the sentence using the following structure:

> *Even if* I had her perky breasts, *I would still* feel embarrassed about my own.

Unpleasant feelings about our bodies result from being disconnected from them and have nothing to do with what our bodies look like. The problem is not your appearance, it is the negative emotions and distorted perceptions of your body.

That's good news because it's typically less painful and much cheaper to change those emotions and perceptions. That's what you're doing by shedding your invisible corset! Unlike a beauty treatment, the results last a lifetime and only get better over time.

FINDING ENOUGHNESS

Never enough. That's what disconnection feels like. Even after I purchased the most technologically advanced skincare serum, applied a full face of high-end makeup, styled my hair perfectly, and managed to get momentarily thin enough, I knew it wouldn't last. I'd get out of the shower, my eyebrows washed off and my hair slicked to my scalp, and I would give into carbs again.

I thought my feelings of *not-enoughness* had to do with my appearance; I didn't know they resulted from body disconnection. That empty, anxious feeling didn't mean I needed to try harder to change my body, it meant I needed to try something entirely different. In *Mere Christianity*, C. S. Lewis notes, "All that we call human history—money, poverty, ambition, war, prostitution, classes, empires, slavery [is] the long terrible story of man trying to find something other than God which will make him happy." All the harm done in the name of beauty is the long, terrible history of women trying to find something other than *connection with our bodies* to make us happy.

The world in which we live does not exist in
some absolute sense but is just one model of reality.

—WADE DAVIS

Yeonmi Park escaped the dictatorship of North Korea, which she describes as a manifestation of George Orwell's *1984*. In her TED Talk, she explains that the reason North Koreans haven't started a revolution against the oppressive regime is partly because they do not know the freedom from which they've been cut off. "If you know you're isolated, that means you're not isolated. Not knowing is the true definition of isolation." In the same way, because we don't realize that we're disconnected from our bodies, we're truly disconnected. We've come to believe this state of body inadequacy, not-enoughness, is *just the ways things are*. But that can be good news because every revolution toward greater freedom began when a few brave souls rejected the idea that *it's just the way things are*.

We can't rise up in revolution when we don't know what freedom is. Freedom is reconnection.

Freedom is when you let the enchantment of the world seep in through your skin, filling you up with softness, magic, and reverence. I may not know what the gifts of your body are, or what particular invisibilities they connect you to. The flower songs? The whisper of the mouse or the murmur of the snake? Maybe it's the untapped poem within the rock, the painting that shimmers in the leaves, the choreography folded into the sunbeam. But what I do know is that the world wants to unfurl its truth within you—within your wonderful body.

CHAPTER FIVE

MACHINE

*To interact with a machine is less complex and
less morally complex than to interact with a community.*

—DERRICK JENSEN

Everywhere we look, our bodies have been turned into a mathematical equation.

"I get anxious if I don't work out," a client recently told me, "because I need to burn off the calories I've eaten. Sometimes I'm tired, and I know it would be best not to push myself, but I think about how many calories I ate and how much I need to burn." Movement, for many people, is no longer an experience of body connection. It becomes a mental calculation that projects us into the past or future and makes us stop listening to our bodies in the present moment. This same dynamic arises around food when we're counting calories, points, or macros: we're not feeling, we're measuring. This is the result of the fourth corset string: mechanization.

AN UNNATURAL HIERARCHY

To understand this fourth corset string, we have to go all the way back to when it first developed in the 1500s with the Scientific Revolution. Although we now see science as independent from religion, the foundation for our scientific paradigm arose from the predominant religious beliefs of those times. One of those beliefs was the existence of a divinely ordained hierarchy, where man was superior to woman, and humans were superior to nature. God sat at the top, and in descending order were angels, kings, priests, men, women, followed by animals. Environmental activist Derrick Jensen explains that this hierarchy "is a profoundly body-hating notion, as according to those who articulated the hierarchy, those at the top—the perfect—are pure spirit; and those at the bottom—the imperfect, the corrupt—are pure matter, pure body."

This hierarchy is, of course, not objective reality. Instead, it's a reflection of the early religious beliefs held by those in power. Religious authority is only as conscious and loving as the humans who wield it, and as history has shown, some highly unconscious and unloving people have used it. This hierarchy served a purpose, acting as a permission slip for men to have ownership of women, and humans to have ownership of nature. A hierarchical perspective contrasts starkly with the worldview held by indigenous cultures across the globe. They perceive nature as a circle of life, where all beings play different but equally important roles, as if we are various organs in the Body of Earth.

From its beginnings, science aimed to control Mother Nature rather than experience the power of connection to her. In the words of René Descartes, considered one of the founders of Western philosophy and science, "I perceived it to be possible to arrive at knowledge highly useful in life . . . and thus render ourselves the lords and possessors of nature." Francis Bacon, often called the father of science, stated, "My only earthly wish is . . . to stretch the deplorably narrow limits of man's dominion over the universe to their promised bounds."

THE DEATH OF NATURE

Until the 1600s, Western philosophers perceived the earth as a living being. Plato compared the earth to an animal, a living creature "comprehending within itself all other animals of a kindred nature."

To Plato, earth was a body with a female soul. Leonardo da Vinci shared the belief of the earth as a living being. He said, "We can say that the earth has a vegetative soul, and that its flesh is the land, and its bones are the structure of the rocks . . . its breathing and its pulse are the ebb and flow of the sea."

Before the Scientific Revolution, the language used to describe the body of the earth and the human body were strikingly parallel because the earth was considered a being. The emergence of science as both a tool of discovery and an establishment, however, killed our Mother Earth in body and soul. Early scientists took a mechanistic view of the universe, likening the earth to a machine. Johannes Kepler was one of the first adopters of this paradigm shift. He said, "My aim is to show that the celestial machine is to be likened not to a divine organism but rather to a clockwork." Galileo Galilei furthered this belief and argued that the world could be understood through mathematical laws. After all, a machine lacks any creativity or free will and is expected to behave predictably.

As the earth transformed from living being into a machine, so did every creature on earth, including the human body. In the early 1600s, Descartes championed the belief of human body as machine. Descartes notoriously cut up living dogs, believing their bodies were mechanistic and, therefore, could feel no pain. When the dogs cried out in anguish, he compared the noise to wind in an organ windpipe—simply the inter-action of the creature's mechanistic body parts. Descartes's comparison of the human body to a machine formed the foundation of Western science and medicine, and eventually calcified into scientific dogma.

The comparison of our body to a machine colors our entire percep-tion. We describe the heart as a pump and the brain as a computer. We gauge our metabolic rate as if we're fueling a machine, considering how many calories we consumed and burned. We eat and sleep and work according to data provided by perpetually conflicting studies or health books, as if someone else has the manual for how best to run our bodies for the most efficient results. Our entire system of Western medicine rests upon the belief that dysfunctional parts of the body can be patched with medication, or removed or replaced with surgery. As with the other corset strings, this paradigm doesn't reflect reality. Instead, this pervasive and largely unquestioned belief is simply accepted as reality.

EXPLOITATION

In her book *The Death of Nature*, Carolyn Merchant explains how the shift from a Living Earth to a Mechanistic Earth created moral consequences:

> *The image of the earth as a living organism and nurturing mother had served as a cultural constraint restricting the actions of human beings. One does not readily slay a mother, dig into her entrails for gold or mutilate her body . . . As long as the earth was considered to be alive and sensitive, it could be considered a breach of human ethical behavior to carry out destructive acts against it.*

We first had to turn Earth from a *she* into an *it* to justify exploitation. This is mechanization: when we diminish or strip the qualities of life from a living being by describing that being as an object.

In order to harm a group of people, one must justify that harm to the general public. As a result, instead of intervening, the mass population will stand aside while this abusive treatment occurs before their eyes. This has been the pattern in every historical event where genocide, enslavement, and brutality were perpetuated against large groups of people. This includes "witches" (independent women and healers) in medieval Europe, Africans enslaved in Europe and America, Jews under Hitler's rule, and indigenous peoples during colonization of their native lands. It includes, also, the human body. We stand aside while we harm our own bodies because we have justified seeing our bodies as machines we own instead of living beings with whom we're in a relationship.

When we see our bodies as machines, we're justified in dominating them. The following analogy, borrowed from author and life coach trainer Martha Beck, illustrates how we fail to see our bodies as living beings. Imagine having a pet dog and running her on the tread-mill until she's panting a hundred breaths per minute. You wouldn't do this to your beloved pet, but we do this to our bodies when we race through our day, fueled by stress and caffeine. Expanding on the anal-ogy, imagine feeding your dog only half the calories she requires for proper growth and development. And when you do feed her, you give her fish food instead of dog food. We wouldn't do this to our pets, yet we treat our bodies this way in our dieting and food choices.

The fact that our cultural mistreatment of our bodies requires us to see them as machines rather than beings is no accident. It is far too lucrative for the beauty, diet, fitness, and medical industries to be a fluke. It is also far too effective a method of female oppression to be accidental. When a culture sees women as objects, all manner of female abuse and inequality is excused. If we unconsciously perceive women's bodies as things, then rape and sexual abuse are more acceptable. If we see her work as merely mechanistic production rather than efforts of a living being, then her work (such as childcare and housework) isn't "real work" and requires no compensation.

SURVIVAL MACHINE VS. LIVING BEING

The opposite of life is not death but to become a ma[chine].

—MONICA SJÖÖ and BARBARA MOR

Science, as a method of inquiry into our universe, is a profound tool for understanding reality and bettering our lives. At the same time, science reflects the level of consciousness, the biases, and the belief systems of those who use it. Consider how at one time the earth was believed to be flat, or that the sun revolved around it. Historically, science has been used to justify racism, the inferiority of women, and homophobia. In the 1800s, for example, ethnology was an accepted field of science purporting that black people descended from a different and inherently inferior group of early humans than white people. And it wasn't until 1973 that homosexuality was no longer listed as a pathology in the American Psychiatric Association's *Diagnostic and Statistical Manual of Mental Disorders.*

While science makes profound contributions to society, it still contributes to bias, exploitation, and mistreatment—particularly of the human body. The following cultural and scientific myths lead us to perceive the body as a survival machine instead of a living being. Many of these myths are unquestioned by science. Only when we examine unquestioned assumptions can we make real scientific progress toward the goals of healing and happiness.

MYTHS THAT MAKE OUR BODIES SURVIVAL MACHINES:	BELIEFS THAT ALLOW OUR BODIES TO BE LIVING BEINGS:
Determinism—our bodies display predictable and pre-programmed behavior	Fluctuation—there exist countless variables outside of our awareness that impact our bodies' behaviors
Reductionism—our bodies can be understood by examining the smallest parts	Relationism—our bodies are greater than the sum of their parts
Materialism—all our body experiences and functions can be explained by molecular and biochemical causes	Expansionism—our bodies function in ways our current scientific paradigm cannot measure or comprehend
Survivalism—our bodies are driven by instinct to pass on genetic material	Potentialism—our bodies are drawn to wholeness and health by a future potential
Isolationism—our bodies exist in isolation	Universalism—our bodies are part of a greater whole

Determinism Says Our Bodies Display
Predictable and Preprogrammed Behavior

Imagine twisting the gear on a windup toy car, then releasing the car on its set of plastic tracks. You expect the car to follow the tracks, and you expect it to travel in proportion to the degree you wound it up.

But what if you held a wriggling puppy in your arms, then put it onto those tiny grooved tracks? You wouldn't expect it to follow the path. You might watch the puppy run off into another room, start gnawing on the plastic pieces of the track, or piddle on the floor. Anyone who has ever raised puppies knows they have free will, curiosity, and unique personalities leading to a wide range of unpredictable behavior. Strangely, however, the expectations we hold of our bodies are more similar to the toy car than the puppy.

We expect our health to thrive if we eat the precise amounts of vitamins, minerals, and macronutrients put forward by the most recent diet. We expect to lose the same amount of weight as the celebrity did, if we follow her trainer's fitness plan. We expect to turbocharge our work habits if we follow the morning routine of the productivity expert. We expect our happiness to skyrocket if we do the same meditation the researcher says changes our brain.

Determinism considers that the human body's reactions are largely predictable by assuming we exist in a *closed system*. A closed system means that we can expect a specific result because we have identified and restricted all the *causes*. Thus, we may expect a certain weight loss diet or supplement protocol to work because we assume certain constants. In reality, countless variables can prove our expectations invalid. For example, our thoughts may impact how much hunger hormone our bodies produce, throwing a wrench in the assumption that we need only to consider calories in and calories out. Stress levels also impact weight fluctuation, regardless of calories consumed.

Even if we take hormones and stress levels into consideration—even if we consider *all* the factors we know to exist within the human body— there are other influential factors we have not yet identified. As recently as 2018, scientists discovered a new organ in the body. Further, it's only been in the last one hundred years that we've been aware of higher frequencies on the electromagnetic spectrum. So what about the dimensions of reality and the aspects of the human body that are still undiscovered?

We expect our bodies to follow the rules because we assume we exist in a closed system. We then feel like failures when our bodies do not behave as expected. We blame our willpower because we believe it's the only variable that could impact our weight loss, fitness, or productivity results.

We More Accurately Reflect Reality if We Reject the Myth of Determinism and Embrace Fluctuation

Embracing the perspective of Fluctuation, we recognize the existence of countless variables outside our comprehension that impact our bodies' behaviors. We understand that holding expectations that our bodies *should* behave a certain way just sets us up for frustration or disappointment. If we were capable of holding *accurate expectations* of our bodies, we would never feel surprised, confused, or upset with them. We acknowledge that what we do know about our universe, earth, and bodies are only drops in the bucket compared to what we do not know.

Stuart Feinstein, professor and chair of the Department of Biological Sciences at Columbia University, sums it up in his book *Ignorance*:

> *Consider the wide stretches of the electromagnetic spectrum, including most obviously the ultraviolet and infrared but also several million additional wavelengths that we now detect only by using devices such as televisions, cell phones, and radios. All were completely unknown, indeed inconceivable, to our ancestors of just a few generations ago. . . . Just as there are forces beyond the perception of our sensory apparatus, there may be perspectives that are beyond the conception of our mental apparatus.*

Reductionism Says Our Bodies Can Be Understood by Examining the Smallest Parts

Instead of considering the human body as a whole, Western medicine and science default to examining the small parts of the human body and ignoring the interconnectedness of every single cell, organ, and system of the body. Indigestion? Take pills to stop stomach acid production. Gallbladder not working? Take it out. Diabetes? Take insulin to fix insulin-resistant cells.

Reductionism attempts to understand the whole of the human body by breaking it down and analyzing the tiniest particles. In his book *Science Set Free*, author and biochemist Rupert Sheldrake points out the primary problem with reductionism: it's like trying to find out how a computer works by grinding it up and studying the molecules of nickel and copper. Sheldrake offers another analogy. He explains how, in his Cambridge chemistry class, he and his classmates "sacrificed" a rat and extracted enzymes from the dead body. Then, they did a series of experiments to examine how those enzymes functioned. He says, "We learned something about enzymes, but nothing about how rats live and behave."

Relationism Suggests We Can More Fully Comprehend Our Bodies, and the Natural World Around Us, Through Relationship

When I was eight year old, I got a pair of pet rats who would be two of my closest companions for the next two years. I watched movies with them snuggled in the pocket of my sweatshirt. I did my homework with them scampering across my desk. I played hide-and-seek with them, searching my bedroom as they found new hiding spaces and waited for discovery. One rat even learned how to undo the latch on her cage and escaped at night to wake me up with a massage of gentle paws on my face.

These rats were more than enzymes, and examination of the atoms in their fur and flesh could not explain their intelligence and unique personalities. My pets were more than the sum of their molecular parts, and I discovered that fact only through relationship with them (albeit not a full relationship, since owning a pet indicates an ownership). In the same way, we're not going to understand the body by merely studying it at a molecular level. We can only begin to comprehend our body's wisdom and intelligence when we connect with it at a relationship level rather than a reductionist level.

Materialism Says All Body Experiences and Functions Can Be Explained by Molecular and Biochemical Causes

The moment you know you do not know is the moment you open yourself to true knowing.

—ERICH SCHIFFMANN

Descartes believed the human mind possesses spiritual consciousness, making humans the only intelligent and conscious species on the planet. He believed our minds are not mechanistic, and are separate from our mechanical physical bodies. This separation of physical matter and spiritual essence is called Cartesian dualism, and provided the foundation for scientific processes until the mid-1800s. This separation created an inevitable conundrum because the body cannot be separated from the mind.

For example, every emotion creates physiological responses. Stress floods the body with the stress hormone cortisol, which alters how the supposedly mechanistic body functions. Falling in love releases the feel-good hormone oxytocin, which improves our health. And, of course, the placebo effect crosses the imaginary separation of body and mind. To work around this challenge, scientific institutions began to write off the existence of mind or nonmeasurable consciousness because it was too spiritual and vague. Matter—measurable atoms and molecules— became the only reality.

Materialism is the belief that all experiences of the human body can be explained by matter alone. This is why, for example, materialistic-minded scientists attempt to explain near-death experiences (reported by nearly 3 percent of the US population) with fluctuations in neurotransmitters or oxygen flow to the brain. They perceive it as "unscientific" that humans might indeed interact with beings of light or dimensions science cannot yet measure. Ironically, it's highly unscientific to insist that human experiences fit into the paradigm of materialism, rather than allowing outlying data to inform the expansion of that limited paradigm.

Expansionism Accepts That the Body Functions in Ways Our Analytical Mind Does Not (and Perhaps Cannot) Understand

When I was seven, my parents purchased a cabin on a wooded island outside Seattle. The first night I slept there, I heard noises that seemed to originate from the wall separating the bedroom from the covered carport. In that carport stood our Ping-Pong table. The noises sounded like the rhythmical thwacking of a Ping-Pong ball, with the occasional skittering of the ball across the table.

I peeked out my bedroom window but saw no one playing Ping-Pong. The sound had stopped, but when I climbed back in bed, it started up again. "It must be ghosts playing," I figured. "That's why I can't see them, and it explains the noise." And then I went to sleep, content with having some explanation, and assuming the friendliness of apparitions who were enjoying a game of table tennis.

It turns out the noise was actually the ancient baseboard heaters—situated on that wall—warming up.

I was trying to understand an observable phenomenon with explanations available to me at the time. I couldn't explain the noise from the baseboard heater because I didn't know such a thing existed—it was completely outside of my mental awareness. It's human nature to understand phenomena with a known explanation instead of sitting with mystery. I call this the Ghosts Playing Ping-Pong Fallacy, and materialism serves as a prime example of this fallacy. It's an attempt to understand the human body with an explanation we presently know. But what if there is a baseboard heater, or other such concepts beyond our present cognition, that we haven't yet considered? What if there are spectrums of reality impacting our thoughts, feelings, and behaviors that go beyond matter?

Survivalism Says Our Body Is Driven by the Instinct to Pass on Genetic Material.

If we believe the body is a machine, how do we answer the question, "Why does the human body exist?" According to Western scientific dogma, the body exists due to an ambiguous evolutionary force described as *survival instinct*. It is one of the most chronic cases of circular reasoning in the scientific world. The logic goes like this: Why does the human body exist? To reproduce. Why does the human body want to reproduce? To pass on genetic material. Why does it want to pass on genetic material? So the human species survives to reproduce further.

Machines only make sense if they have designers.

—RUPERT SHELDRAKE

Survivalism suggests that species survive and evolve only to effectively pass on genetic material, without any higher purpose. Sheldrake identifies the breach in logic here: "[Materialists] cannot prove that all evolution is purposeless, they assume it." It is possible, after all, that our body expresses itself and evolves for the purpose of creativity, connection, and/or love. Sheldrake points out another misassumption.

A machine *presupposes* an intelligent force that created it. A machine cannot create itself from a void because it is built with an intended final result. A purpose was imagined, and then an intelligent force assembled pieces with function in mind. The pieces of the human machine could not randomly assemble by themselves.

Potentialism Suggests the Body Is Drawn to Wholeness and Health by a Future Potential

Have you ever felt the potential of something or some experience that exists in your future? You long to make this potential real, and so you make choices to direct your life toward that potential. You sense it like a shadow cast on your present from a future event, you might even glimpse it on the horizon of your life. Perhaps this is a possible new relationship, or a career you can't fully envision but where you'll feel fulfilled.

In the same way, the body is drawn toward a future potential. Aristotle described this concept with the term *entelechy*. The entelechy of an acorn, for example, guides it to grow into an oak tree. The philosopher and mystic Tielhard de Chardin used the phrase "the lure of becoming" to describe this invisible force.

When a human embryo develops in the womb, it undergoes the process of cell differentiation. What starts out as the union of an egg and sperm cell becomes a complex being. Cells replicate, and then some cells turn into lung tissue, some turn into heart tissue, and some turn into brain tissue. The instructions for this process aren't in DNA. In fact, we have no idea how the cells know how to differentiate and assemble themselves.

Materialistic science lacks any explanation for how an acorn knows how to become an oak tree, or how an embryo knows how to develop into an adult. Yet survivalism dogma insists living beings are driven by an evolutionarily programmed survival instinct. This instinct is used to explain why the natural world exists yet has no future goal or higher purpose. Survivalism presupposes rather than explains away purpose because it rests on the assumption that there is an innate drive to exist and reproduce.

Isolationism Says Our Bodies Exist in Isolation

Imagine the windup toy car again. If the windup gear on that single car breaks, the repercussions would not noticeably impact anyone or anything else. The toy is tossed into the trash without a second thought and is replaced with a newer model.

When we perceive the body as a machine, we assume it to be an independent object. We believe what happens to our bodies is an isolated event, affecting our experience but not the world around us. As an extension of that belief, we consider our bodies our own private property. We assume we can do with our bodies what we wish, impacting only our lives and not the world around us.

---

*We misperceive the world if we see it as
individuals struggling against one another.*

—MARGARET WHEATLEY

Universalism Acknowledges the Body Is Part of a Greater Whole

No part of our body acts in isolation from the rest of it, and neither does our body act apart from our whole environment. Consider an example from Western medicine: if a patient has heartburn, he usually receives a prescription drug that reduces the production of stomach acid. This is an attempt to fix a "broken part" of the human machine. The medication often alleviates the pain associated with heartburn but can create additional health issues. When stomach acid production is reduced, we cannot properly digest food and often experience further bloating, constipation, and nutrient imbalances.

Our digestive system is a part of our body—it affects every part of it, and every other part of our body affects it. In the same way, humanity is one system in the Body of Earth. We affect every other part of our earth. The other systems and organs and cells in the Body of Earth affect us. Our bodies do not exist in isolation, and any choice we make about them sends a shiver, however minute, across the entire web of life. Like it or not, we are all in this together.

Every aspect of the human body communicates—the brain signals the digestive organs, hormones send messages to organs, and sensory information from the skin travels back to the brain. Hair follicles are different from muscle fibers, yet they're all connected via the communication systems within the body. In chapter 4, I spoke about the lineage of healers who crafted remedies by listening to plants. Could this be possible because we are all part of the same communication system within the Body of Earth?

In an Instagram post, bestselling author Elizabeth Gilbert shared a snapshot of a journal entry where she scribbled, "CITY OF GIRLS [her book] is to be your medicine—frothy, easy, frivolous + a gift. We will make this one as easy as possible, but only if you agree to do the same." Along the inside margin of the same page, she wrote "I AGREE." In the caption, she explained that she didn't know who gave her this message, who the "we" was, and why she agreed.

I scrolled down through the comments to where one woman had posted, "This is all very unscientific." To which Elizabeth replied, "Thank you, sweetheart! You're right!"

I hear flowers speak and sing to me. And I believe all animals, vegetables, and minerals who share the Body of Earth speak to each other somehow. Some people tell me, "That's all very unscientific." I tell them, "Thank you, sweetheart! You're right!"

THE BODY'S INNER COMPASS

The benefit of perceiving our body as a survival machine is we are then justified in our control of her. We can make her go without sleep and fuel her with only caffeine and sugar. We can slather her with chemical-laden personal care products and fill her with chemical-laden foods. We order new parts for her at the cosmetic surgeon's office. We can refuse to listen to her and use substances and indulge in habits that numb out her voice. We can do all this without moral conflict because this is appropriate treatment of an object.

But we have to ask: By turning our bodies into machines, what are we losing out on? Consider the story of the dentist turned nutrition anthropologist, Dr. Weston A. Price.

In the 1930s, Dr. Price embarked on a mission that would take him across the globe. He wanted to discover the secrets to straight, strong, healthy teeth. He visited tribal communities in all parts of the world, from Eskimos and Native Americans in North America to indigenous communities in South America, Polynesia, and Malaysia, aborigines in Australia, Maori in New Zealand, tribal groups in Africa, and village communities in Scandinavia.

At the time of his travels, there still existed indigenous communities untouched by Western influence, where individuals followed the diet and lifestyle of their ancestors. In these communities, the inhabitants' nutrition had remained relatively unchanged for thousands of years. Dr. Price took a systematic approach to his research, comparing the health of these isolated people with communities that had incorporated Western foods. For example, he studied a group of aborigines who lived apart from Western influence, and compared them to a group of aborigines who ate Western foods like refined flour, pasteurized milk, and white sugar.

Dr. Price found that the indigenous communities who adhered to the diet of their ancestors had strong, straight teeth with negligible levels of tooth decay. The communities where Westernized foods were eaten, however, struggled with chronic tooth decay and crooked teeth. Dental health wasn't the only difference. The indigenous communities who honored their traditional diets radiated health. They had symmetrical bone structure, easy pregnancies, complication-free births, emotional stability, and no evidence of degenerative disease. They also had no need for eyeglasses or orthodontia, as eyesight problems and oral issues stem largely from generational nutrient deficiencies, which cause structural problems with our facial bones.

Life in all its splendor is Mother Nature obeyed.

—WESTON PRICE

When indigenous communities started to eat refined foods, however, their communities began to look a lot more like what we think of as normal. Children started to exhibit crowded teeth and poor eyesight. Birth challenges and defects appeared due to the structural problems related to nutrient deficiencies. Chronic diseases like allergies, asthma, and arthritis manifested.

Struck by the physical health of the non-Westernized indigenous cultures, Dr. Price analyzed their diets. "What were they doing right?" he wondered. "Are there commonalities in their diets?" Dr. Price found that, although the ancestral diets had different ingredients based on geographical location, the nutrient profile of these diets was strikingly parallel. While macronutrient (carbohydrate, protein, and fat) levels varied, the levels of vitamins and minerals were similar and significantly higher than the levels found in modernized diets. Further, ancient cultures all followed strict and sacred nutrition protocols for couples who planned to conceive. Indigenous peoples also followed similar food preparation techniques, such as fermentation.

Thousands and thousands of years ago, our ancestors across the globe followed a lifestyle and diet that allowed health to flourish.

They managed to land on similar vitamin and minerals levels, even though they obtained nutrients from vastly different sources. They knew which nutrients needed to be increased during pregnancy to ensure optimal bone development of their babies. And they did all this without measuring devices to monitor the nutrient content of their food, or peer-reviewed, placebo-controlled nutrition studies. Our ancestors relied on their bodies' guidance to tell them what to eat, and how much, just like our ancestors relied on the plant songs to tell them how to make medicines.

Mechanization of the body wasn't an accident; it was an extension of the belief that humans are entitled to own and control nature. But if we're controlling our bodies, how can we communicate with them? How can plants and animals and the earth communicate with us? Control precludes a relationship, and communication is only present in relationship. Love, also, exists only in relationships of being-to-being, not being-to-machine. It's time to ask yourself: Is the possibility of love worth giving up control?

CHAPTER SIX

COERCION

*The measure of a man's estimate of your strength
is the kind of weapons he feels that he must use
in order to hold you fast in a prescribed place.*

—HOWARD THURMAN

The idea that women are choosing to deplete their resources through beauty practices results from the catastrophic misunderstanding that force can only be applied through physical means rather than psychological means. Mind control, coercion, manipulation are all forms of force that are equivalent to physical force. This psychological abuse, although often invisible, can be even more damaging than its physical counterpart. For the very reason the abuser is *not* holding a gun to our head, we often see the abuser as our friend or helper. That means we trust them, defend them, and ultimately allow them to do us more harm.

Dr. David McDermott, a researcher of cult dynamics and brainwashing says:

> *In mind control there may be no physical coercion or violence, but it can actually be much more effective in controlling a person. That's because coercion can change behavior, but coercive persuasion (mind control) will change attitude and behavior. And the "victim" is happily and actively participa[ting] in the changes, believing it is best for them!*

The beauty industry is a psychological abuser of global proportions. Because this abuse scars our minds rather than our bodies, it goes largely unrecognized. But psychological abuse bruises the psyche just like a fist bruises flesh, and emotional pain engages the same part of the brain as physical pain. Still, we turn to makeup to give us confidence, we adhere to diet rituals to feel worthy, and we undergo plastic surgery to feel sexy and desirable. We seek from our abuser the very thing it intentionally stripped from us: a fundamental sense of adequacy as women and as human beings. We give this industry the power to build us up, and by extension, we give it the power to tear us down.

The $500 billion beauty industry controls not with a visible gun held to our head but through invisible warfare. Small as we may seem compared to this gargantuan industry, we hold the power to reclaim our health, peace, and confidence. That's because the beauty industry does not get its power from the handful of individuals who are CEOs of beauty corporations. No, this beast is fed and fattened by every woman who hasn't realized her choice to feel at home in her body.

Each day, through a million automatic thoughts and actions, we provide the beast its life-force. We feed it our time, energy, money, and—the nutrient it requires to thrive—our fear. We've enabled the force that is hurting us. The fabled patriarchy isn't out there—it's inside us. That's the disturbing part: the magnitude of our own responsibility for our pain. But there's also a glorious part. At this moment, we can take back that power for ourselves. We can avail ourselves of the resources we've used to create something so deathly, ugly, and destructive to create something equally as life-giving, healing, and beautiful.

ARE WOMEN CHOOSING THIS?

I purchased my first bottle of eye cream at age sixteen because, after reading various articles in women's magazines, I learned that it was most effective to prevent, rather than treat, wrinkles. Months prior to walking into Sephora, I scrolled through endless online product reviews and analyzed the recommendations of various beauty gurus on YouTube. Finally, I had settled on a cream from a preservative-free luxury brand. In the Sephora store, the cashier swiped my debit card, and it was done. I had spent eighty dollars of the money I earned from after-school babysitting and working weekends at a gift shop. I had exchanged the equivalent of eleven hours of my time for half an ounce of some precious elixir that would, hopefully, delay the onset of the normal human aging process.

That evening, after washing and moisturizing my face, I gently tapped the cream around the orbital bone with my ring finger, just as I had watched the YouTube beauty gurus do, as they glowed under expert lighting. The cream smelled heavenly, floral and light, as it kissed my skin like cool satin. At the same time, however, an acrid fear gathered in the pit of my stomach. I gazed into the mirror, studying the smooth adolescent skin around my eyes. I thought, "I cannot change. I am not safe here, in this body."

I consider myself at sixteen an intelligent and self-possessed young woman. What compelled me to spend eighty dollars of my hard-earned money on a shiny jar of eye cream? Even as I began to question beauty culture, I thought it was my own weakness that I felt less than human without makeup on, and I believed my body insecurity stemmed from my own lack of mental resilience. "Nobody is forcing beauty products and cosmetic procedures on women," I thought. "Women are choosing this."

That's what I believed until the fifth and strongest string of the invisible corset became visible to me.

At the age of twenty-one, I found myself in the waiting room of a locally renowned nutrition and energy work practitioner. Charismatic, disarming, and looking a decade younger than his fifty-nine years, he ushered me into his treatment room. I became a snake under the gaze of a snake charmer, absolutely entranced as he began his client intake interview. After a few sessions, he said I was energetically gifted, and would I like to see him outside of a session to talk about this. He noted he didn't extend this offer to other clients. Feeling honored and assuming this to be an opening for a mentorship or friendship, I accepted an invitation to go to his house. There, he initiated sexual contact—and I didn't say no. My thoughts moved like tar, and my body felt miles away as he moved his hands up my shirt, then down my pants. I was asking myself, "Did I agree to this? Do I want this? Is this okay because it's someone I trust?"

I agreed to start a relationship with him. From day one, he peeled back the layers of my self-worth and self-trust in order to influence my behavior. He knew how to wield his criticisms so they sliced right to my soul, confirming what I most feared about myself: that I was inadequate and inherently unworthy. And I believed him. It would take nearly three years before I realized the psychological grooming and manipulation tactics he employed to influence my choices.

Then, I discovered I was one in a long line of students, clients, and colleagues he had put in the same position. We came together and came forward, trying to find solid ground when it felt like the rug had been pulled out from under our feet. We systematically analyzed our shared experience in order to reverse-engineer his playbook. That's when I realized: the exact same tactics he used to control our sexuality, energy, and finances were the same tactics the beauty industry uses to accomplish the same result.

PSYCHOLOGICAL ABUSE

My abuser used the same techniques of psychological abuse that beauty culture employs on a mass cultural scale. I experienced a microcosm of the macrocosm. In a psychologically abusive relationship, no matter a woman's age, race, religion, or location, she will likely be impacted by five coercive mechanisms. In this section, I personify the abuser with the pronoun "he" for brevity, but be aware that a psychological abuser can take the form of any gender, race, association, religion, corporation, institution, or other power structure.

The abuser leverages an unequal power dynamic.

Cultural patterns of abuse reveal a high concentration of abusers (which can include men and women) in positions where their authority is unquestioned because they seek out and leverage those positions. This was evidenced by the #MeToo movement, when the curtain rose to show how culturally respected men used their money, status, and position to harm others who lacked those forms of power.

The same goes for women and beauty culture: we assume the information and guidance we receive from various authority figures, such as celebrities or skincare research, has our best interests at heart. A psychological abuser will insist, "I know, better than you, how you should live your life and what decisions you should make." We fail to realize the vast amount of financial bias and incentive at play, and underestimate the abuser's desire to manipulate us.

The abuser strips your confidence so he can parse it back out, on his own terms, and for his own benefit.

A psychological abuser knows how to dismantle his victim's confidence, so the victim is left in a state of paralysis. The intention is to create wounds, or leverage existing wounds, and then offer the only salve that can sooth the searing pain of his criticism.

Beauty culture takes the same approach, pummeling us with messages that we need to fix, correct, cover, and disguise any way in which our body deviates from an impossible beauty standard. At the same time, we earn compliments or a boost in confidence from a new mascara or pricey facial. Beauty products and procedures seem to temporarily relieve the pain inflicted by the beauty industry in the first place.

The abuser systematically leads you to distrust yourself.

Psychological abuse leads you to devalue your reality and emotional experience, particularly when your emotions might lead you to realize your mistreatment. For example, if you are angry with an abuser, he might say you are irrational and selfish. His underlying message is, "You can't feel or trust your emotions." Psychological abusers also warn you that you'll do irreparable harm to yourself or your loved ones if you make your own life choices. The underlying message is, "If you trust your intuition over my authority, you'll sabotage yourself and those you care about." Does this sound familiar?

Women receive cultural messages that we are not to be trusted to navigate our lives. Our emotional response is too much, too little, too prolonged, too abnormal. Our gut feelings are irrational. And if we express our True Selves, or reveal our true bodies, we'll sabotage our families, relationships, career, and social status.

The abuser keeps you sleep deprived and stressed.

When I began researching psychological abuse, I was shocked to read that psychological abusers often intentionally exhaust their victims. I suddenly recognized the ways my abuser fabricated false emergencies, provoked disagreements, and prolonged arguments long into the night to make me sleep deprived and anxious. In that running-on-empty state, I was too exhausted to tune in to my intuition and recognize abusive patterns.

Cultural messages create the same impact. Women feel like we lack enough hours in the day to maintain a perfect home, family, body, and career because we *do* lack enough hours. The only way to keep up with societal standards of perfection is to exhaust ourselves, run on caffeine, and lose out on sleep. The more exhausted a woman is, the more difficult it is for her to see clearly.

Her body shifts into fight-or-flight mode, the nervous system's emergency response. Stress hormones flood her body, increasing her blood pressure and heart rate. In this state, she'll likely struggle with anxiety, insomnia, and poor digestion. Her intuition also diminishes. Our gut feelings are relayed to our brain through the vagus nerve, which is like a telephone cable between the brain and organs. Fight-or-flight, however, diminishes vagal nerve function. In a depleted and agitated state, she's less likely to perceive her own exploitation and manipulation, and she lacks the energy to break free from a cycle of psychological abuse.

The abuser leads you to distrust other women.

When I first met with the other women targeted by my abuser, I felt hesitant. "Will they believe me?" I wondered. "Or will they hate me?" After all, my perception of them was clouded by what our abuser said. He managed to exploit many women at a time from a single community by pitting us against each other. "She secretly hates you. You shouldn't bother talking with her," he told me of a colleague. And of another, "She's unstable, keep your distance."

If women in our culture compare notes about our experience in our bodies, we'll reach a similar conclusion. We'll learn that beauty culture has made us distrust each other on purpose. Beauty culture tells us that if we tell the truth about being in our bodies, other women will judge us instead of saying, "Me too." Only by telling the truth will women realize we aren't each other's competition but our salvation. If women fear each other, we'll never recognize the patterns of psychological abuse that keep us trapped. Historically, women strapped each other into corsets, binding each other tight enough to bruise ribs. As long as women distrust each other, we will continue to restrict each other in invisible corsets. It's time to untie each other.

COERCION VS. CONSENT

Consent is the ability to make a decision with free will, and free will exists only if we can make a decision without the influence of fear. Leveraging fear, including guilt and shame, is a manipulative strategy to influence someone's choice. Sadly, we exist in a culture where fear is so frequently used to control other people's behavior, we don't recognize it as a form of manipulation. For example, many children are raised in religions that tell them they'll go to hell unless they live according to a specific rulebook. If these children comply out of fear of eternal damnation, they have not chosen their lifestyle out of free will—they've been coerced into a set of behaviors and beliefs.

In the same way, women are not consenting to the diets, beauty practices, and procedures that harm our mental and physical health. When it comes to any sexual assault, as well as beauty culture's victims, consent is not a matter of, "Did she say yes?" But rather, "Could she have said no?" Are women able to say no to disordered eating, if we've been coerced to equate our self-worth with thinness? Are we able to say no to Botox, when we've been coerced to believe that looking young is critical to our professional reputation? Are we able to say no to makeup, when we've been coerced to believe that we are inadequate in our bare skin? Saying yes out of fear, guilt, or shame is *never* true consent.

For Harvey Weinstein, and the other men called out in the #MeToo movement, it wasn't really about sex. It was ultimately about exerting their power and control over women. In the same way, when it comes to the beauty industry, it's not really about how thin we are, how large our breasts are, how hair-free our labia are, or how Botoxed our foreheads are. It's not about beauty, it's about controlling women's time, money, and emotions. It's about maintaining power over women's bodies, because those who do not trust the immense power of our bodies will always try to control that power.

IT IS THAT BAD

When I came forward about my abuser, I faced a cacophony of voices telling me, "It's not that bad." Some of my colleagues, for example, feared my abuser's incrimination would prove harmful to their own careers, by damaging the reputation of the institution that accredited us. Some of his fellow teachers, in their desire to see their long-time friend as innocent, outlined the ways this situation was my fault. Those messages paralleled the arguments that insist it's women's fault for wearing the invisible corset: "You chose this. You're an adult not a child. You could have said no."

"It's not that bad" is the reasoning that perpetuates the continuation of mass psychological abuse of women at the hands of the beauty industry. Eating disorders may lead to the highest death rate of any mental illness, but it's not bad enough to make headline news. Chemicals in cosmetics are linked to cancer, but it's not bad enough to make the FDA change ingredient safety standards. A girl's self-esteem plummets at puberty, but it's not bad enough to implement widespread changes in our media and education system to protect girls' self-esteem.

In an interview on Oprah's *SuperSoul Sunday*, Oprah and Reese Witherspoon discussed their experience in psychologically abusive relationships. In response to the question, "What's the most difficult decision you've had to make to fulfill your destiny?" Reese replied, "Leaving an abusive relationship." She explained how a line was crossed, and she knew she had to leave the psychologically and verbally abusive relationship. Then Oprah shared her own similar experience. She explained that, as a child, she had watched a close female relative being physically beaten by a partner. "I'll never let somebody hit me," she vowed at age ten. Then, in her twenties, she found herself in a psychologically and verbally abusive relationship. When her partner slammed a door on her hand, she saw herself in a mirror, and she suddenly realized, "I had become that woman who had allowed myself to be psychologically, verbally assaulted and there was no difference between that and being actually hit."

Women trust the beauty industry as a friend, turning to skincare products as a form of self-care. We believe a beauty product or procedure will give us the confidence to achieve success in our education or career. We confuse the diet industry with a healthy lifestyle. We find solace and companionship in YouTube tutorials that teach us how to sculpt, contour, and highlight our face. But if we look at the overall impact of the industry, not just the good intentions of many who work in it, we realize that the beauty industry is not women's ally but an enemy in sheep's clothing.

Our culture tends to recognize physical abuse, not psychological abuse, even when the effects are the same. Imagine what would happen if fourteen-year-old girls were put in a jail cell and starved, provided with only half the nutrients required for their growth and development. Individuals from every walk of life would recognize this for what it is: abuse. So why don't we recognize the abuse taking place when media images and cultural messages psychologically coerce fourteen-year-old girls into starving themselves? The means are different, but the results are the same. The intention is the same too: our culture does not want adolescent girls to be free.

Even if women are not physically dying from our culture's psychological abuse, our souls are dying. In an abusive relationship, the victim cannot live her own life because she is under the control of the abuser. She carries out his desires and demands, often unknowingly, in an effort to self-protect and survive. When we strive to achieve the beauty standard, we are not fulfilling our own longings or pursuing our souls' purpose. Instead, we are simply pawns in the hands of our abuser.

VICTIM BLAMING IN BEAUTY CULTURE

On social media, women sometimes tell me, "I wish I had your confidence and bravery to accept my body. I know I should be mentally stronger." I didn't achieve body acceptance by pondering the inadequacy of my self-esteem and mental resilience. Instead, I asked the same question that allowed me to escape my abusive relationship: "Why is my abuser—beauty culture—so effective and insidious that it undermines the most powerful and self-determined women among us?"

The "it's not that bad" mentality makes beauty culture a breeding ground for victim blaming. When we fail to recognize psychological abuse, we tend to transfer the blame from the abuser to the victim. For example, we often assume something is wrong with a woman if she copes through emotional eating. A narrative embedded in our mind says, "She has some character flaw that made her susceptible. If she really wanted to, if she tried harder, she could get better." If a woman undergoes plastic surgery, we might think, "She's weak in some way if she succumbed to the pressures of beauty culture." Or if a woman feels ashamed without makeup, we might tell her, "Don't be so self-conscious!" All these reactions place 100 percent of the blame on women instead of also exploring the abuse of power by beauty culture.

Fundamental attribution error, a concept discussed in every Psychology 101 class, suggests that when we consider someone else's behavior, we tend to blame their character not their circumstances. This is internal attribution. How often do you do this with your friends or partner when they behave in a way that irks you?

You may think, "My friend is late again. She's always late to our dates. She's a disrespectful person."

But when we consider our own behavior, we usually default to external attribution. If we run late, we blame circumstances rather than our character: "I couldn't help being late. I spilled my coffee, and then I got stuck in traffic, and I had to send an important email before I left."

To some degree, the body positivity movement tends to make internal attributions and shift the responsibility of *the abuser's behavior* to *our personal character*. We hear the message, "Love your body in the face of an artificial beauty standard! Just be mentally and emotionally strong enough not to be impacted!" It's similar to telling women, "If you don't want to get sexually assaulted, wear conservative clothes and don't drink alcohol." It's not the woman's fault when she gets assaulted, it's the assailant's. Similarly, it's not due to a character flaw when women hate our bodies, it's the only expected outcome of our abusive culture.

LEAVING THE ABUSER

When I've been on the outside of abusive relationships, I've looked in and thought, "Why doesn't she leave him? Can't she see he isn't going to change, that she will always be unhappy with him, and that he'll keep hurting her?" But when I was on the inside of this dynamic, I thought, "I can't leave, I need him." Women remain in the psychologically abusive relationship with our culture because we believe we need the abuser.

We believe we need our beauty to dictate our self-worth. Otherwise, where does our self-worth come from? We believe we need to compete to be more attractive than other women in order to be enough. We believe we need to hate ourselves in order to improve ourselves. We are addicted to allowing someone else to describe who we are and, therefore, prescribe our lives.

Every woman has a well-stocked arsenal of anger potentially useful against those oppressions, personal and institutional, which brought that anger into being.

—AUDRE LORDE

In order to remain in an abusive relationship, we must repress our anger. Anger is a force that recognizes and seeks to protect our self-worth. It's the fuel that can mobilize us out of self-destructive environments. Every woman who remains in the psychologically abusive relationship with beauty culture has repressed her anger. How can we not be angry when we're told that the things we have little control over, such as the aging process and our body features, make us less valuable? How can we not be angry when we feel obligated to spend time and money on our appearance when men do not? How can we not be angry when we watch our daughters succumb to body hatred, and we feel powerless to stop it? If we weren't repressing our anger, we would march through offices, malls, places of worship, and homes with a megaphone saying, "Attention all sentient beings: this is so wrong."

We have to get angry enough to save ourselves and our daughters. Anger acknowledges how much we have been harmed, generation after generation. It recognizes that this harm was done intentionally, not accidentally. It concedes the reality that we're watching our daughters and granddaughters suffer debilitating body insecurity that stifles their potential and sometimes cuts their life short. Yet we've avoided diving into the depths of our rage because we believe we can't handle it. If we go there, would we ever surface again? Would we lose our sanity?

As long as we house an emotion that we're afraid to feel because we don't think we can handle it, we believe we can't handle ourselves. We remain afraid of ourselves. Fully reclaiming our power requires that we walk into the fire, feel the flames, and discover the part of us that cannot be burned.

AN EYE FOR AN EYE

Anger mobilizes us, acknowledging our mistreatment so we can leave toxic situations. By recognizing the harm done, anger seeks to create justice. Anger tends to want revenge, an eye for an eye. "I want you to feel what I felt," anger says, "so that you recognize what you did. And so this hurt in the world can stop." Achieving revenge, however, requires that we hold on to the pain so we can deal it back out. Revenge never breaks the cycle of pain because it perpetuates the energy that harmed us. It also keeps us in an unhealed position—fearful that if we let our eye grow back, then we lose the validation to take the abuser's eye.

> There is a time in our lives, usually mid-life, when
> a woman has to make a decision—possibly the most
> important psychic decision of her future life—and that is,
> whether to be bitter or not.
>
> —CLARISSA PINKOLA ESTÉS

We are free when we choose redemption instead of revenge. Redemption means we grow back the lost eye, so we can better see how to serve others and create a just world. We use our pain and we move through the anger, but we don't hold on to it.

EXERCISE: Anger Alchemy

The following ritual moves you through anger to redemption of the abuse inflicted by beauty culture.

Gather a group of women (two is enough for a group!). Have everyone bring a disposable object that represents the abuse of beauty culture. Some ideas include a women's magazine laden with toxic headlines, a blank check representing the money spent on products, or compression undergarments representing the pain we endure to be beautiful.

First, place the objects in a corner of the room, and orient yourselves so you are in a semi-circle facing these objects. Each woman should have a pen and paper. Instruct everyone to speed write to the prompt: "There was anger in her because ____." What does your anger need to express? How has beauty culture hurt you? How have others hurt you because they were trapped in the invisible corset? Set a timer for seven minutes while everyone writes. Remember, speed writing means you keep your pen moving, disregarding grammar and the voice of your inner critic, to allow the subconscious to spill its guts.

When the seven minutes are up, take turns reading your work to the abuser as if it were a person. Provide each woman space to share without interruption. You might nod, clap, or snap your fingers, to show your support, but give her the floor. When she has said (or cried, or screamed) her piece, she places her hand on the shoulder of the next woman to indicate it is her turn.

Next, gather up the items in a trash bag, and toss them out, ritualistically discarding the abuser.

Then, crank the speakers and play your favorite fuck-you songs (I recommend: "Fuck You" by Lily Allen, "Fuckin' Perfect" by Pink, "Send My Love" by Adele) and dance. Dance the rage, grief, and empowerment through your body.

Lastly, get paper and pens again, and reset the timer for seven minutes. Now, each women writes a letter to a young girl, one whom she either knows or doesn't. It could be her daughter or granddaughter, a mentee, a student, or patient. This letter is not written with the intention of being shared with the group, but it can be if that feels healing to the writer.

Start with:

> Dear [Enter name or description here],
>
> For you, I am letting go of the pain. For you, I am going to discover the freedom, joy, and confidence that are possible in my body so I can show you how to get there too.

Then, tell her the pain you want her to avoid, and the positive experiences you want her to have in her body. What do you need to tell her, from your own experience, so she is equipped to avoid the abusive relationship you previously found yourself in?

Wish her all the best, send her your love, and sign the letter.

Take this letter home and refer to it when you find yourself struggling to reject the abuser's opinion. Let the letter remind you that you are escaping the cycle of abuse for your sisters, daughters, and granddaughters. You are doing it for the entire family of women.

LEAVING FOR MORE LOVE

When our self-worth depends on an abuser's approval, our self-worth is *conditional*. In beauty culture, we must meet certain beauty conditions in order to feel good about ourselves. In contrast, *essential* self-worth arises when we know we are loved for who we are, without wearing a disguise or telling lies. When you leave abusive beauty culture, you get to reject the criticism of your body. You no longer need to care about your body being called fat or wrinkled. But if you stop valuing the criticism, you must also stop valuing the praise.

Power can be taken but not given. The process of taking is empowerment in itself.

—GLORIA STEINEM

Beauty culture's praise and criticism are the same thing. They both reduce your value to your appearance. This means your value is how much time and money you perpetually invest in the improvement project of your body, coupled with your luck in the genetic lottery. The praise, therefore, isn't really a compliment. And it's certainly not love.

It's a risk, leaving behind the approval of beauty culture when it's the only form of love we know. But it's not real love. Only by rejecting the opinion of beauty culture can you give yourself the chance to be loved for the truth of you.

PART TWO

CUTTING

THE

STRINGS

Now that we've identified the invisible corset strings, we can start the great unlacing of the beliefs and perceptions that kept us trapped.

CHAPTER SEVEN

LISTENING

Listening moves us closer, it helps us become more whole,
more healthy, more holy. Not listening creates fragmentation,
and fragmentation is the root of all suffering.

—MARGARET WHEATLEY

Imagine being in a long-term partnership or marriage and never discussing your partner's future goals and dreams. Instead, you proceed as
if your desires are all that matter, and your partner exists only to support
you. When they try to bring to your attention the one-sidedness of this
approach, you shut them down. "Not now, I don't have time to talk
about this," you might say, or "Your opinion is ridiculous, I simply can't
be bothered with it." You may even say, "You're annoying me with all
your human needs and feelings. Can you just be a quiet and acquiescent
object in the background of my life?" We wouldn't expect a relationship
like that to be healthy, happy, or enduring. Yet, when we're trapped in
the invisible corset, that's how we relate to our bodies every single day.

THE WILLINGNESS TO BE WRONG

I learned the adage "You can be right or you can be happy" applies to
my relationship with my body. Happiness in any relationship requires

truly listening to our partners, but for years, the fear of being wrong kept me from listening to my body. As it turns out, though, the best thing I ever was was wrong.

For example, I used to think that Western medicine was the only way to manage my ulcerative colitis, an autoimmune disease. When I was eighteen, my doctors told me that, because medications had failed, my last remaining option was an invasive surgery to remove a portion of my intestine. I believed them and felt devastated. Shortly after receiving this news, however, a book called *Breaking the Vicious Cycle* seemed to jump off a bookshelf at me. It outlined a dietary protocol that had helped others with my disease. My doctors had always told me, "Nutrition won't really help," and "This is an incurable disease." But as I held that book, a small voice rising from the core of my body said, audibly but faintly, "I have to try this."

I chose to listen to that inexplicable voice. Within three days of my new diet, my chronic pain and internal bleeding stopped. Three months later, with careful attention to my nutrition and stress levels, I tapered off all medications and avoided the surgery. This "impossible" healing had always been available to me, but it was on the other side of being wrong about the uselessness of nutrition. The price of impossible healing, it turns out, is being wrong.

I had refused to listen to my body for years because listening is the act of losing control. To truly listen to someone, we have to be willing to lose control of our perceptions and expand our perspective. Listening to our bodies means we allow our beliefs and values to be changed based on our bodies' feedback. I look back and consider why I resisted this opportunity for a radical perspective change, given how exhausting it was to see my body as an enemy rather than a soulmate.

I knew, deep down, that listening to my body would require that I give up certain cultural values and, instead, challenge those toxic values. Oh, the vexing inconvenience of that! I didn't want to *grow*, I just wanted to be liked. I wanted everyone who adhered to culture's definitions of successful and beautiful to see me as successful and beautiful. For example, as a young teen, I desperately wanted the approval and recognition that academic success bestows. I didn't realize that culture doles out approval and recognition primarily to those who treat their bodies like machines rather than living beings.

Believing that I couldn't rest or play until I had "made it," I fueled my academic endeavors with anxiety and adrenaline. I frequently pushed my body over the edge and landed in the hospital with autoimmune flare-ups. I refused to honor my fatigue and ignored my longing to enjoy the present moment. By denying myself rest and play, I was withholding necessary nutrients from my body. As I've learned to tune in to my body, I know that the lavish inclusion of these activities supports my physical, mental, and spiritual health—aspects that the body values more than accomplishments.

Yes, it's uncomfortable to be confronted with an aspect of ourselves that we don't like, but we can't change what we refuse to see.

—ROBIN DIANGELO

By living according to culture's definition of success, I was harming the most significant relationship of my life—the relationship with my body. I had, in fact, turned my body into a trophy wife. She was an object for me to use, someone to visibly prove my status, someone who existed only to serve my ego rather than inspire my spiritual growth. Beauty culture requires us to live a lifestyle and make choices that run counter to the wisdom within our bodies. So, in order to continue our day-to-day life, we need to shut down feedback from our bodies. In the long term, we're sabotaging our health and contentment. In the short term, however, we're avoiding the inconvenience of aligning our goals and values with our lifelong partner. We think we can have it our way. But is it really going our way?

When we're trapped in the invisible corset, we long to feel relaxed, joyful, and confident in our bodies. But this healing remains unavailable to us while we remain within that limiting belief system. We can enjoy the unshackled confidence, magnetism, allure, and self-celebration we dream about; we just have to be willing to be wrong that the solution is product, diet, or beauty procedure. We have to be willing to be wrong in thinking that our bodies are the ones that need to change, and realize that it's our minds we need to change. The willingness to be wrong is the only way to listen to your body, and listening to your body is the only way to heal your relationship with her.

Fundamentalists are those who refuse to entertain the question, "What if I'm wrong about what I believe?" There are religious fundamentalists, scientific fundamentalists, and political fundamentalists. These people want to be right more than they want to be healed or happy. As a result, they shut out, shut down, and shut off any perspective that could widen their own. Talking to them often feels like butting your head against a wall or being on the receiving end of heavy-duty gaslighting. When it comes to the invisible corset, there are beauty fundamentalists. These individuals, of whom I was one, won't give themselves the chance to be free of the corset. They don't believe they can accept the unaltered truth of their bodies, and they doubt that other people can too. They refuse to accept feedback from their bodies, and even gaslight their own bodies by rejecting their discomfort and intuition in order to conform to beauty culture.

This chapter is for women who are willing to be wrong, who are even willing for that to be a wonderful thing. That willingness holds courageous self-love. It opens the doors for you to welcome in your body's voice, the inner wisdom that knows how to heal you and knows how you can heal the world. And our world needs that, desperately. We need women rising up all over, saying, "I'm willing to let my body show me how my culturally indoctrinated perceptions, beliefs, and values are wrong. I'm willing to live, instead, from the wisdom inside of me."

EMBRACING CURIOSITY

The first step in listening to your body is to embrace curiosity. This mindset shift allows us to open our inner ear to the body's feedback. The opposite of curiosity is defensiveness, a barricade we establish against our intuition and inner wisdom.

Relationship experts John Gottman and Nan Silver explain that defensiveness is a way of saying, "It's not me, it's you." They consider defensiveness one of the four qualities in a partnership that predicts divorce. When it comes to the relationship with our bodies, the same holds true: we cannot achieve a fulfilling partnership when we've dug our heels into defensiveness. When we're telling our bodies, "The problem isn't me, it's you," we lose the opportunity to gain awareness of our blind spots and our unintentionally harmful behavior.

We can only be redeemed to the extent which we see ourselves.

—MARTIN BUBER

When we embrace curiosity, a state of interested receptivity, the mindset shift allows us to open our inner ear to our bodies' feedback. Instead of defaulting to, "Our relationship problems aren't my fault, body!" we entertain the question, "Hey body, how can I improve things between us?"

Here are three ways to embody a curious mindset rather than a defensive one so you can listen to your body.

Accept Humility, Not Entitlement

Entitlement rests on the assumption that our needs are more valid and important than someone else's. We believe we have a right to have things go our way, no matter the sacrifices or consequences for other people (or our environment as a whole). When it comes to our bodies, we often feel entitled about our weight and appearance. We may believe, unquestioningly, that our bodies are obligated to meet our ideal weight and that we deserve to have bodies that match our culturally conditioned definition of beauty. We may undergo surgery, extreme fitness routines, and obsessive food habits in order to achieve our "ideal" body. But what if our bodies don't want to undergo such stressful routines, and hold a different opinion about their preferred shape?

Humility allows room for the perspective of others. It's not the belief, "I don't know anything," but rather, "I don't know everything. What a relief!" We make room for the possibility of more ease and support with the wisdom of our bodies, which ultimately means more ease and support with the universe. Humility allows the world to grow into a gentler, kinder place. With an entitled perspective, we insist on our right to dominate. With humility, we give up that exhausting fight.

Turn Rigidity into Flexibility

Defensiveness often masquerades behind the statement, "That's just how I am." I used this phrase routinely when I was trapped in the invisible corset. I used to always spend thirty minutes doing my makeup because I needed to always look my best and "that's just how I am." I needed to be ballerina-thin because I was a dancer and "that's just how I am." I needed to breathe in toxic nail polish fumes so that my manicure was always flawless because "that's just how I am."

In reality, I was saying, "I am just trapped in the invisible corset—that's just my identity." Identification with roles, hobbies, and appearances often feels grounding because it provides structure and community to our lives. But with that structure comes limitation, and with that community can come a fear of rejection. Flexibility means entertaining the question, "What if it's okay to change?" Posing this question to yourself invites your subconscious mind to entertain new possibilities for your expansion and freedom.

Move from Denial into Responsibility

Can you think of a time when you shut down an inkling or a gut feeling, only to have it later validated? Maybe you felt suspicious and raised your concerns about a partner's mannerisms when they were on the phone, only to be told, "You're acting insecure and paranoid. Why don't you trust me, given everything I've done for you?" Later, you discovered they were cheating on you. Maybe your gut tells you that something is wrong with your workplace, but management says, "Your wellbeing is our highest priority!" Later, you discovered that management practiced favoritism or unethical workplace decisions. In situations like these, we tend to deny our instincts and intuition because trusting ourselves means changing our behavior instead of waiting for someone else to change theirs. When we take responsibility, we accept our ability to respond.

To move from denial to responsibility, check in with the areas of your life that feel most uncomfortable. Look for instances that make you feel tight, agitated, or anxious. These feelings are how your body tells you, "You're denying my wisdom." Then consider if you are blaming someone else for your discomfort. Are you telling yourself it's the fault of your child, partner, parent, boss, government, or community? Even if those individuals or institutions are creating discomfort, they do not have the ability to make you happy. That wisdom is found within you, and later in this chapter I'll give you tools for accessing it.

EXERCISE: Put Yourself in Your Body's Shoes

Consider three interactions where you've been on the receiving end of the forms of defensiveness that were just described. Go through your lifetime and pick out an instance where you gave feedback to someone, but then they expressed entitlement and told you, "That's just how I am," or denied your perspective entirely. Journal about these instances and explore how they made you feel.

Now, with those experiences fresh in your heart and mind, consider how you might be showing those same three types of defensiveness toward your body. Write these down and ask yourself: "What might my body be feeling about being on the receiving end of this?"

RELAXATION

If you wanted to have a deep and meaningful conversation with your partner, how would you establish the space for it? You might send them a text letting them know you want to connect with them that evening, then arrange for a quiet night in. You might consider how conversation between you often feels easier in nature, so you arrange a time for a hike and ask that they be emotionally present for the conversation. You'd likely find that a quiet, private environment, along with giving them a heads-up, would facilitate the most effective and fulfilling conversation. The same applies when we listen to our bodies.

The more relaxed and calm we are, the better our bodies communicate with us. As noted earlier in chapter 4, our nervous system has two states: parasympathetic, often called rest-and-digest, and sympathetic, also known as fight-or-flight. The parasympathetic state facilitates communication between our body and brain by activating the vagus nerve. This nerve acts like a telephone cable, relaying messages from the brain and the digestive system, lungs, and heart. This body-to-brain connection is one pathway that intuitive gut feelings are translated into conscious thought. Stress and anxiety trigger the sympathetic state of the nervous system, however, and reduce vagus nerve function. In this way, stress limits your ability to be in touch with your intuition and listen to your body.

In fact, a sympathetic state reduces our ability to feel *everything*: emotions, physical sensations, pain, pleasure, sexual arousal, hunger, and satiety. For this reason, we can get addicted to stress the same way we get addicted to drugs. A sympathetic state generates stress hormones called adrenaline and cortisol, which have the same effect as caffeine and anesthesia. We often keep ourselves stressed out because we've become reliant on these hormones to numb and energize us. The downside is that this short-term gain comes at the expense of our longevity and well-being. When we keep our bodies pumped up on these stress hormones, we throw other hormones out of whack, contributing to painful periods and infertility, causing digestive and mood problems, and impeding the body's healing processes.

If we're afraid of being wrong and want to remain in the invisible corset, we often use stress as a strategy to avoid listening to our bodies. You might be using stress as a silencing mechanism if you:

- keep yourself running around the clock

- feel irrational fear or guilt about napping or resting

- avoid taking time off, or fill your vacations with intense activity

- find yourself facing mini-emergencies whenever your life is about to slow down

Our bodies always communicate with us. But when we're constantly stressed, that communication is more painful and inconvenient. It often takes the form of chronic health problems that escalate into burnout, physical breakdown, or chronic illness. We make our bodies a much more comfortable place to live when we learn to listen to them before they need to use pain to get through to us.

When we don't create the time and space for relaxation, we are saying to our bodies, our partners, "It's simply not a priority to listen to you. Everything else is more important. It's not that I can't listen to you, it's that I don't want to." Simply setting aside ten minutes a day to practice being in a calm, parasympathetic state establishes better communication possibilities between you and your body.

EXERCISE: Parasympathetic Practice

Set a timer for ten minutes and find a quiet, solitary space. This may be sitting in your parked car or lying on your bed—wherever you can find ten minutes of alone time.

Close your eyes and bring attention to your breathing. Allow your belly to fully expand with your inhales, and exhale slowly through your mouth—a long, extended exhale activates the vagus nerve. Notice if you feel your heart rate slowing down. Feel your body melting onto the surface supporting you. Keep your attention inward and notice any physical changes that occur as you breathe deeply. Do you notice any sensations on your skin? What does the inside of your head and belly and chest feel like? Shifting attention to what it feels like in your body is active listening.

Do this exercise at least once daily, and use it additionally when you feel most anxious or overwhelmed, particularly when you feel that you *don't* have ten minutes to spare. You'll be surprised that you may find this routine more soothing and effective than reaching for other stress-coping mechanisms, such as mindlessly scrolling through social media, reaching for food, or drinking alcohol. (If you wish to use it, I've created a ten-minute audio meditation to use for this exercise. You can find it at InvisibleCorset.com/guidedrelaxation.)

You may also consider Floral Song flower essences to support parasympathetic function and to shift patterns of stress held in the body. See the appendix for further details.

TECHNIQUES FOR BODY LISTENING

In my coaching practice, I use two simple techniques to help my clients tune in to their body's voice. These daily practices are exactly that: practices. Accessing your intuition is not some magical, inherited quality bestowed by the genetic gods upon a select few. Instead, getting in touch with your body's voice is like playing the piano.

At first, you sit down at the keyboard and plunk out coarse notes. Then, with practice, you develop such muscle memory that you can play certain songs with your eyes closed. Your sense of hearing also expands, and you become attuned to nuances of tone you previously couldn't discern. The same phenomena will happen when you practice accessing your intuition. You'll develop new muscle memory, widen your senses, and learn to perceive the subtleties of how your body speaks to you.

Before I equip you with these powerful techniques for body listening, I'll address three common hesitations that often arise. When my clients and students raise the following concerns, I tell them, "That concern is normal and part of the process of trusting your body for the first time! You have a choice. You can use that concern as an excuse to procrastinate and not listen to your body, or you can recognize the fear as old programming and choose to move forward anyway."

1. "I'm afraid of making mistakes."

    If you're afraid of making a mistake while learning to play the piano, you'll never put your fingers on a keyboard. When it comes to listening and trusting your body, ask yourself this question (posed to me by one of my intuitive teachers): "What if there are no mistakes, just practice?"

2. "I'm not getting a clear response from my body."

    Would you expect to play a Mozart sonata perfectly the first time you sat down at a keyboard? It's an unrealistic expectation to perfectly discern your body's voice through these exercises in the beginning. While we may occasionally get sudden intuitive messages, more often, it takes repeated practice to clearly hear your body. Part of the practice is to trust what you're receiving. Soon, your answers will become clearer and clearer. But the only way to clarity is to make your way through the doubt.

3. "These exercises feel so unnatural and even uncomfortable to me. Am I doing them correctly?"

If you watch experienced piano players, they close their eyes, sink into the music, and let their fingers fly across the keyboard. What you don't see is the times they cried at the piano bench, ripped up their music in frustration, or hit the keys so hard the piano went out of tune. (Or was that just me?) Every time I hear a woman tell me, "Lauren, these intuitive practices are just too uncomfortable for me. In fact, I wonder if I'm even capable of doing them," I hear her say, "I don't think the outcome is worth feeling uncomfortable right now. My discomfort with doing something new is currently louder than my desire to bring new, wonderful experiences into my life." It requires practice to make listening to your body feel easy and natural. It's only a matter of that practice being worth it to you.

Are you ready to start tuning in to your body's wisdom?

EXERCISE: Getting a Body Yes and Body No

In this exercise, you're going to learn how your body says yes or no to life situations or choices. First, you establish a baseline feeling of yes and no. The sensations are initially exaggerated so you can get a really clear idea of the feelings.

Before beginning the exercise, read through the instructions first. (Alternatively, listen to the audio at InvisibleCorset.com/bodyyes.)

Take a few deep breaths into your belly, inhaling through the nose and slowly exhaling through the mouth. Feel your muscles melt and relax. Then, close your eyes and start to see yourself in a safe place. Follow where your imagination leads—this can be a space in nature or inside. You feel the pure air around you. Everything feels comfortable.

Envision two doors in front of you, one is your "Yes" door and one is your "No" door. Put all your attention on the "No" door as you begin to have a sense of what's behind it. You know that this door is a portal to a room filled with sights, sounds, and smells you find hideous. You know that as soon as you open the door, you will be smacked in the face by a foul smell that makes your stomach turn. Insects or animals you dislike might come forward at you, and the air in the room will feel humid and hot, or clammy and cold, and will make your skin crawl. Get clear about seeing what's behind that door. Now, imagine yourself walking toward it. Place your hand on the doorknob.

As your hand touches the knob, notice what you feel in your body. How does your breathing change? What do you notice in your muscles, particularly your shoulders and abdomen? What are the sensations you feel as you get close to the horrors behind this door?

Once the sensations are clear and strong, without opening the door, turn around and walk back to a neutral spot.

Now, imagine what's behind your "Yes" door. You know that as soon as you walk through, you'll be enveloped by air that is your exact favorite temperature. It may smell like your favorite scent—freshly baked cookies, a summer garden, or your favorite perfume. You know the space is going to be filled with a golden light that feels like pure love as it touches your skin. The door may lead to a space inside or outside, but wherever it is, it looks and feels like heaven. You might even find a loved one or special animal behind the door, waiting for you.

Now, walk toward the "Yes" door and place your hand on the knob. How does it feel in your body, knowing you are about to step into heaven? What happens to your breathing, the feeling in your belly, your muscles? Do you feel a temperature change within you or any sense of light in or around you?

If you wish, you can open the door to allow the sensations to intensify. You now have a clear idea of what your body's yes feels like.

I encourage my clients to get a body yes or no for different areas of their lives where they're facing conflict or indecision. To do this, I have them close their eyes and envision a choice they're facing. I tell them, "Imagine yourself saying yes to this choice. See yourself moving forward with it. Now, take your time to feel into your body. Do you have the same yes sensations you felt when you established your body yes? Or does it feel more like a no?" You can do the same. Set aside a few quiet, relaxed moments and envision a choice or situation. Does your body say yes or no to it?

LISTENING THROUGH WRITING

In the classic novel *1984*, the main character, Winston, starts journaling—an illegal activity in his authoritarian country. His mind drifts while he is writing. After daydreaming, he looks down at his paper and realizes he has written "DOWN WITH BIG BROTHER" over and over. Winston had never before let those words form in his conscious mind. Doing so would be a form of "thoughtcrime" in his dystopian country. By allowing his unconscious mind to take control of the pen, he channeled the voice of his body. It was his intuitive knowing: the truth in his bones.

Nineteen Eighty-Four is a study in the control mechanisms used in a fictional dystopian world, but these same control tactics are used in the real world to convince women that our bodies are to be feared instead of trusted. Just as in the novel, women's history has been stripped from us, so we are without knowledge of our past freedom. Our male-centric language lacks adequate words for the breadth of women's experiences. And while we don't have Big Brother watching us, we've internalized the gaze of other people, and we seek to make our bodies acceptable to their perception. Our conscious minds may be indoctrinated with lies, but our bodies, like Winston's, know the truth.

Through writing, we can discover intuitive wisdom that we've blocked from our conscious mind. We can also discover things our body knows that we don't know. For example, in the documentary *Embrace*, Renee Airya, a body image activist, shared her profound experience of writing her body's wisdom. One day, when journaling, she wrote, "Something is really wrong with you and you're going to die." After writing that, she stopped and put a question mark next to the statement. Shortly after, she went to the doctor for an examination and learned she had a brain tumor. The tumor was removed, leaving her with partial facial paralysis. The whole experience sparked her journey of supporting healthy body image.

Like Winston and Renee, I've accessed my body's wisdom through writing. During a journaling session years ago, my pen flew across the page as I processed the relationship I was in at the time. Suddenly, I wrote "I'm done" on the page. It shocked me, as I perceived the relationship as enduring, but I stared down at those words, and the truth in them made my hair stand on end. Wanting to repeat this self-discovery, I implemented a simple exercise that allowed me to get in touch with my body's voice. The more I practiced this process, the more wisdom came through. As I've guided my clients and students through this writing process, they've uncovered their own profound, intuitive realizations.

EXERCISE: Writing Your Body's Voice

Reach for your journal or notebook, and each time you do this exercise, title it "A Letter From My Body." I've found it critical to handwrite this exercise rather than use a computer. When I'm on a computer, I tend to default to my editor mode because it's easier to delete words. For this process to work, you must be completely unfiltered. Set a timer for five minutes, and write, at the top of the page:

> *Dear [Your Name],*
> *This is your body and this is what I want to tell you.*

Then, write to yourself from the voice of your body. A frequent refrain I hear is, "I have so many voices in my head, and I don't know which one is coming from my body!" You don't have to know, because this is a *practice*—just like practicing an instrument. Even if you doubt what you're writing, keep writing. The only way to fail at this is to not do it.

Keep your pen moving for the entire five minutes. The secret to allowing your body's intuitive voice to come through is to write faster than your inner critic and faster than your hesitation. Above all, do not allow yourself to stall because you have writer's block. Writer's block is typically a made-up scapegoat—the more accurate term for it is *control*. If you need to, you can keep your pen moving by writing something like, "Keep going, honey," or, "You can do this, just keep writing!"

Lastly, when the timer dings, sign the letter, "Love, Your Body."

Now, it's time for listening. Reread what your body just told you. You'll find that much of what you've written is messy and incoherent, but this is part of the process. Just consider it as hitting the wrong notes on the keyboard as you are learning a piano piece: it's inevitable. A sentence is never wasted because it was necessary practice. As you read your writing, you'll find it studded with jewels of wisdom. Underline any section or phrase that stands out for you.

Incorporate this writing technique into your daily morning or evening routine.

SHE WOULDN'T ASK YOU
IF YOU COULDN'T HANDLE IT

Recently, an idea for a novel sprang into my head. I've heard various authors and artists claim that ideas have a life of their own and choose their collaborator, and I agree. This idea grabbed me in a bear hug from behind as I stood on a street corner, spun me around, and said, "Hey, wanna make something grand together?" Having identified myself as a nonfiction author, my first response was, "Well, idea, I'm delighted to meet you, but are you sure you've picked the right person for this job?" The idea considered me suitable, however, as a few months later, I met the main character from the story.

One afternoon, I woke up from a nap feeling this character distinctly knocking inside my head. Dazed and semiconscious, I grabbed a pen and my favorite notebook and began writing. As if taking dictation from this character, I scribbled as fast as I could without any idea of where we were headed. I felt her in the room, invisible and resplendent, breathing with me. When I finished a page of writing and titled it "Prologue," I heard her say, "That's all for now. There will be more later." I blurted out loud, "What? I hardly know what this story is about, and this prologue doesn't make sense to me! How am I supposed to do this?" Before she dissolved from the room, she replied, "Darling, I wouldn't ask you if you couldn't handle it."

In her book *Feel the Fear . . . and Do It Anyway*, Dr. Susan Jeffers explains that the root of all fear is the concern that we can't handle what we are afraid of. For years, I was afraid to listen to my body's voice because I was afraid I couldn't handle what she would tell me. I knew she would ask me to change my life, leave certain relationships, start hard conversations, and set boundaries. The thought of those things made my stomach drop to my feet. So, believing I wasn't capable of improving my life, and unwilling to be wrong, I smothered her voice and clung to control.

In the same way this character knew my potential, even when I doubted it, your body knows what you can handle. Yes, your body will tell you some difficult things. Some things you may have been trying not to hear. But when you know you can handle it, it doesn't have to be easy—and when it doesn't have to be easy, it can be magnificent. And *you* deserve magnificent.

CHAPTER EIGHT

DISCOVERING YOUR TRUE SELF

I had started to see myself, and once you start
to see yourself, you cannot pretend anymore.

—IJEOMA OLUO

Imagine that your parents, caretakers, teachers, or other loved ones sit you down for "a talk" when you are about six years old. This is what they say:

> *You face an important choice, one that will impact the rest of your life. It's the decision to discover your True Self. Your True Self is the part of you that is happy, creative, and playful. Your True Self not only makes your life wonderful, but it is also essential to the people, animals, and plants that are struggling right now on Earth. Your True Self will bring important healing to the world, even if you don't understand how. The discovery of your True Self is filled with surprises, excitement, and celebration. Because this discovery is a lifelong process, it just gets better as you grow older.*
>
> *Some people don't choose to find their True Self, and they live as a False Self. They're very unhappy on the inside, even if their life looks perfect on the outside. They might be popular, but they don't*

experience real love or friendship because they don't let love inside themselves. They tend to have a lot of health issues because their body is allergic to their False Self. They kind of hurt all the time.

It feels much better to be your True Self, but you need to know one thing: it takes courage. Courage means you live with your heart. So you'll feel a lot of love in your life: love for nature, animals, your work, your friends, your family, and even people you don't know. Your heart gets hurt, though. Being your True Self means that sometimes you feel pain. But you'll have enough love, friendship, and joy in your life to heal that pain, no matter how much you're hurting.

As your True Self, you will shine. You will do magnificent things. You'll inspire others, just like you feel inspired by other people. Your life can be quiet or it can be loud, whichever way you like it. You can dress any way you like, even if nobody has looked that way before. You can celebrate and love your unique body because it's not supposed to look like anyone else's body. You can be absolutely anything you want to be, even if no one has been it before. It will take courage and strength, but you have everything you need inside you. You will love being yourself.

Do you want to choose to be your True Self?

Most of us aren't presented with this choice when we're young. Instead, we develop False Selves because it appears to be the only viable survival option. Fortunately, this choice is always ours. To discover our True Selves, we first have to identify our False Selves and where they came from.

THE CULT OF BEAUTY

A friend of mine was born into a cult religion. She remembers how, at age eight, she started questioning her religious teachings. Upon hearing a religious leader declare women's inferiority to men, she thought, "That's not fair." Her big questions about God and life got her labeled as "challenging." Her questions were continually met with responses of, "That's just the way it is," or, "Because God said so." She began to tamp down her intuition—the part of her that whispered, "Hey, this doesn't feel right."

She learned that, in order to be accepted into her community, she had to develop a False Self to silence and hide her True Self. She turned her strength against herself.

She controlled her True Self so well that her False Self became the perfect believer, wife, and mother.

She controlled her intuition, her doubt, and her feelings of rage and grief at the inequalities perpetuated by the cult. She controlled her critical thinking skills, her curiosity, and her truth. Then, at thirty-six, she saw her own daughter following in her footsteps, absorbing the toxic messages. Her intuition broke through the walls she'd built around it, and the biggest, loudest "No!" rose up within her. "This is *not* happening to my daughter," she thought. "I am out of here." She realized that the only way she would find freedom and give her daughter that freedom was to let her True Self break through. This required the scary steps of releasing the control around her inner voice and tamped-down emotions.

The cults' lure is, if you just come along, all will be fine,
and everyone will live happily ever after.

—MARGARET THALER SINGER

When we hear the word *cult*, we might think of a group of white-robed individuals chanting around a fire, or religious fundamentalists who cut themselves off from electricity and modern conveniences. Most cults, however, exist unseen and integrate themselves in our daily lives. One such cult is beauty culture. Like my friend, we've been born into a system that insists on our inferiority, sells us salvation (through buying products), and offers asinine explanations of why this is the case—instead of "It's God's will," we default to "It's biology!" In this environment, we develop a False Self and lose touch with our integrity and soul purpose.

To understand why we live in a beauty *CULTure*, consider the five primary characteristics of cults.

1. **The group unquestioningly accepts one ideology as law.** In beauty culture, we internalize the idea that we must be beautiful to be worthy, loved, and accepted. It doesn't matter if we're successful in other areas of our lives. We've come to believe that we're less acceptable if cellulite mars our thighs, pimples speckle our face, or childbirth left behind stretch marks and softened flesh.

2. **Doubt in the ideology is punished.** When individuals publicly question the belief that women are obligated to look beautiful or hot, we provoke a backlash. We often incur the criticism that "we've let ourselves go," which is exactly the point—we've let ourselves go free of beauty culture's lies.

3. **Shame and guilt are leveraged to ensure obedience of members.** Consider how tabloids shame women's bodies, or how the diet industry provokes guilt about eating to convince us to purchase diet plans, products, and subscriptions.

4. **The group is preoccupied with making money.** Beauty culture exists to control women's spending behavior, and therefore control our socioeconomic power. But this underlying prerogative is disguised by the offer to help us feel better. Beauty culture promises, "I can make you happy, fulfilled, *enough*."

5. **Members are expected to devote inordinate amounts of time to group activities.** What happens when we spend all our free time on ten-step skincare routines, fitness regimens, and watching makeup tutorials? We don't have the time to discover *who we truly are*.

THE FALSE SELF

Mystics, psychologists, and psychoanalysts have used the term *False Self* to describe the masks we wear to hide our true character, desires, and gifts. This mask consists of behaviors and personality traits that conflict with our True Selves—the aspect of us informed by and connected to divine wisdom. The vigilance and energy required to maintain our False Selves often leads us to develop anxiety, depression, and harmful coping mechanisms. The False Self doesn't simply arise, however. It's a response to manipulative strategies employed by cultural systems and community leaders.

Every one of us is shadowed by an illusory person: a false self.
This is the man that I want myself to be but who cannot exist,
because God does not know anything about him. And to be
unknown of God is altogether too much privacy.

—THOMAS MERTON

Psychologist Edgar Schein studied the brainwashing techniques that Chinese Communists used against American prisoners. He identified three steps that distanced prisoners from their identity, integrity, and independence.

1. **Unfreezing** refers to uprooting the individual's present beliefs. They develop self-doubt and are receptive to new ways of understanding. In beauty culture, this occurs around age nine, when girls leave the partnership with their bodies.

2. **Changing** the personality involves installing a new belief system. Because the individual's perception of reality has been shattered or dissolved in the previous unfreezing phase, they are highly susceptible to swallowing new ideas without critical analysis.

This process involves repetitive indoctrination of new concepts, as well as reward and punishment to condition behavior.

3. **Refreezing** occurs when the new belief system is adopted as normal, rather than new. The individual's new values and identity may be in direct conflict with who they used to be.

Our False Selves develop in response to numerous cultural and familial influences. Beauty culture installs aspects of our False Selves because our True Selves are incapable of the self-harm, self-hatred, and financial self-sabotage required to uphold the beauty industry. Our False Selves can be manipulated, our True Selves cannot. Whereas the True Self acts from truth and love, the False Self sees these universal forces as a threat to its safety. It cannot trust the truth, for it is protecting itself against reality. We often cling to our False Selves because they offer a survival mechanism when we believe who we really are poses a threat to our wellbeing and belonging.

REUNITING WITH OUR TRUE SELVES

What happens when we escape beauty culture's control over us? We find out who we truly are underneath our False Selves, and three beautiful qualities emerge: self-honesty, self-prioritization, and self-belonging.

Self-Honesty

A mother takes care of everyone but herself. Is it a coincidence she develops chronic fatigue syndrome and becomes cared for by her family, instead of being the caretaker?

A woman feels disconnected from her partner and craves his listening and empathy. Is it a coincidence that she develops an ongoing yeast infection that gives her an out from having sex?

An executive hates her job, but she is afraid to make the transition into a more fulfilling career. Is it a coincidence she develops an autoimmune disease and is forced to slow down?

In her memoir, *Love Warrior*, Glennon Doyle recounts her adolescent stay in a mental hospital when she struggled with bulimia. She remembers looking at a patient with self-harm scars running up her arms, thinking, "That's how she tells the truth," just like Glennon herself told the truth by throwing up in the toilet. Glennon reflects on the fact that their families considered most patients insensitive liars when in fact they were "ultrasensitive truth tellers." She said of these sensitive people, "We saw everyone around us smiling and repeating 'I'm fine! I'm fine! I'm fine!' and we found ourselves unable to join them in all the pretending. We had to tell the truth, which was: 'Actually, I'm not fine.' But no one knows how to handle hearing that truth, so we found other ways to tell it."

> *All truths wait in all things.*
>
> —WALT WHITMAN

Our bodies speak the truth for us. No matter how much we resist it, try to hide it, or ignore it, the truth always exists. When we withhold truth from the world, our False Selves employ unconscious self-harming strategies to cope with the pressurized force of truth inside us. Self-harm extends beyond what we typically consider it to be, such as cutting, substance abuse, and eating disorders. It encompasses any unhealthy mental or behavioral patterns that we inflict on ourselves unconsciously.

Anxiety is largely a form of self-harm, for example. While anxiety may not be a choice, the behaviors, expectations, and beliefs that create it likely are a choice. When women leave toxic relationships or the abusive expectations of beauty culture, their anxiety level typically takes a nose dive. In the same way, eating problems such as binging or emotional eating may not be a choice. The life stressors and unaddressed traumas that can contribute to food issues, however, typically are a choice. When a woman invites radical self-honesty into her life, she realizes that many of the problems she faced were symptoms of her body telling the truth for her. By stepping into her True Self, she makes her body a comfortable place to live.

Self-Prioritization

One of the most nerve-racking periods in my business was when I realized I was going to have to financially invest in it for it to grow. I hadn't faced discomfort when I had invested in a previous business, an LLC that I co-owned. It was unnerving to invest only in myself because no one else would shoulder the blame if I didn't see a financial return, and no one shared the responsibility of venturing into uncharted territory. I also realized that investing in myself this way was true self-care because, although it would require an immense measure of self-trust, I was giving myself the chance to create the future lifestyle and income I wanted. Self-prioritization, the act of investing in our True Selves, presents the same opportunity.

The truth is always the answer.
It's rarely comfortable, but it's always the answer.

—ANNE LAMOTT

"I give too much," many of my clients say. "I give so much to my kids, my partner, my clients, my students. I just feel exhausted and at the end of my rope." As women, we're conditioned to believe in the self-sacrifice equation. The calculation goes like this: "The less I take for myself, the more I can give to others. The more I can give to others, the more they'll like me. If I take more for myself, I'll feel guilty because I'm taking away from them, and I'll also feel insecure because they won't like me. Therefore, the less I take, the more I'll be liked, and the more I'm liked, the safer I am." We subconsciously use this mental math in our relationships with partners, kids, friends, and colleagues. But in the words of Dr. Phil, "How's that working out for you?"

Germaine Greer analyzed this phenomenon in her landmark feminist treatise *The Female Eunuch*. "For so much sacrificed self the expected reward is security, and seeing that a reward is expected it cannot properly speaking be called self-sacrifice at all. It is in fact a kind of commerce," she writes. We're using self-sacrifice as our currency, but instead of buying security, we're filling our shopping bags with resentment, exhaustion, and frustration. That's because self-sacrifice serves only our False Selves. Ironically, our False Self is of the least service to other people. This is particularly pertinent for those in wellness, coaching, or therapy careers, because only our True Selves can facilitate healing in others. When one woman chooses to self-prioritize, she sets off a positive chain reaction that reaches far beyond her sight.

Self-Belonging

Can you think of a time when you dressed, acted, or spoke in a way that betrayed your True Self? Maybe you wore clothing that your family or partner preferred, even though it didn't feel right to you. Perhaps you purchased accessories with flashy designer labels to fit in, even though you didn't see the point of it. Or you might have toned down your vibrant clothing style because this expression felt out of place. With any of these choices, we're trying to find belonging within a community. However, because we're rejecting our True Selves in the process, we'll never experience the connectedness we desire. Even if other people accept us into their tribe, clique, or group, we'll never experience true acceptance when others are interacting with our False Selves.

A sense of belonging arises when we show up as our True Selves and, in that way, contribute to the wellbeing of other people. That meaningful, impactful connection to others nourishes the soul in a way that being seen as popular or desirable cannot. Many people achieve an outwardly successful life yet feel empty inside because they feel like they're not truly contributing to other people. Their self-indulgent life appears to them ultimately meaningless, and they feel unrecognized for their True Selves. We seek external validation and approval to fill the void of true connection. But when we participate in the human family, both taking and giving in a way essential to the whole, we don't need other people's approval because we have a sense of belonging. The False Self thinks, "I need people to like me," while the True Self says, "I feel connected to other people."

We are truly aware of our own worth only when we feel
that our existence and behavior are beneficial to the community,
that is to say, when one feels "I am of use to someone."

—ICHIRO KISHIMI AND FUMITAKE KOGA

In Disney's *The Lion King*, adult Simba faces the choice to return to his homeland, where his family suffers under the evil rule of his uncle Scar. One night, when he feels most conflicted and utterly separated from his family, a vision of his dead father, Mufasa, appears in the stars above him and says, "You have forgotten who you are and so have forgotten me. Look inside yourself, Simba. You are more than what you have become. You must take your place in your circle of life."

When Mufasa's spirit says, "You are more than what you have become," he means that Simba's powerful True Self lies beneath his self-doubt and feelings of isolation. Our valuable contribution to others—our unique gifts, personality, and presence—comes from our True Selves, but our False Selves separate and isolate us from others. In order to participate in the circle of life, to give and receive from others in such a way that we feel connected, we must remember *who we are.*

TRUE SELF-CARE

I used to think self-care was a ten-step skincare routine or a pedicure while I flipped through a woman's magazine. It's a reasonable misunderstanding, given how much the beauty industry profits by telling us self-care means using beauty products. In reality, self-care involves the rebellious act of uncovering our True Selves. It's creating a life that takes care of you, where you can relax into, and celebrate, your authentic self.

Redefine Self-Comfort

In my work as a nutrition consultant, I noticed many people who struggled with autoimmune issues often improved greatly by eliminating gluten from their diet. Unfortunately, they perceived this dietary change as intolerably outside their comfort zone. Yet these individuals were far from comfortable, as their disease symptoms included chronic pain, digestive problems, autoimmune disease, and skin issues. Their comfort zone would be better described as an uncomfortable-but-familiar zone. This is where the False Self likes to live. The True Self prefers the free-but-unfamiliar zone.

Caring for myself is not self-indulgence, it is self-preservation, and that is an act of political warfare.

—AUDRE LORDE

My friend is a powerhouse financial advisor. Analytical and intellectual, her personality fits her career perfectly. For much of her life, she kept her health care within analytical and intellectual confines, veering away from anything she thought was woo-woo. Then, she began to feel drawn to alternative means of wellness, such as acupuncture and energy medicine. She faced internal resistance, because adopting these tools would mean giving up control of how others perceived her. She didn't want to be perceived as woo-woo—by herself or others! But the longer she stayed in her comfort zone, the more she cut herself off from powerful tools to support the wellbeing of her mind, body, and spirit. Ultimately, she decided she could be more comfortable and somewhat-woo.

More often than not, we remain in an uncomfortable zone from fear of how others will perceive us. Ultimately, this is not because we care about what other people think, but rather because we don't want to handle our own discomfort around someone else's perception of us. In other words, *there's no such thing as people pleasing*. Anytime you stifle your True Self to gain approval and validation from another, you are doing so to please your False Self—not them.

EXERCISE: Finding Your Comfort Zone

Consider an area in your life where you're remaining uncomfortable because you don't want to deal with someone else's perception of you.

For example, maybe you're not setting a boundary because you're afraid to be called "rude." Maybe you're not speaking your feelings because you're concerned they will get defensive. Maybe you're not changing your employment or relationship situation because you're afraid to be considered irresponsible.

For this exercise, follow these steps:

1. Write down one phrase you're afraid others will think or say. It might be something like:

   - What if they think I'm being x? (For example: What if they think I'm being rude?)

   - What if they tell others y about me?

   - What if they say I'm z?

2. Then, in a move inspired by spiritual teacher Byron Katie, swap out "they" with "I":

   - What if I think I'm being *x*?

3. Write three reasons why this isn't true.
   What if I think I'm being rude?

   a. It's not rude to prioritize my True Self.

   b. It's not rude to set a positive example of boundary setting for my kids.

   c. It's not rude to take myself out of toxic environments.

4. Finally, write down the opposite of the previous statement:
   What if I think I'm being polite?
   Write three reasons why this could be the case.

   - I'm being polite to my True Self by putting her first.

   - I'm being polite to my body by supporting her health.

   - I'm being polite to the person I'm setting a boundary with because now we can have a more honest relationship.

Self-Enjoyment

"Wouldst thou like to live deliciously?" This is the question the devil asks the adolescent girl, Thomasin, in the final minutes of the 2015 film *The Witch*. Thomasin stares at him, her eyes wide and lips parted in disbelief. "Yes," she replies, and agrees to sign the devil's book. Given only this scene, one may wonder why this young Puritan woman knowingly sold her soul to the devil. In the scenes leading up to this climactic moment, however, he had targeted his vulnerable and isolated victim, stripping her life of pleasure, comfort, and community. In so doing, he became her only hope.

"If you've made a deal with the devil, it's probably because no one else has offered you more favorable terms," writes M. E. Thomas, in her book *Confessions of a Sociopath*. Women have made a deal with the devil because no one has offered us better terms. We've agreed to create False Selves and repress our true wisdom and uniqueness. We've agreed to fight and alter and dominate our bodies because we're told that's how we achieve happiness, love, and acceptance. We're told delicious is on the other side of suffering.

We've dutifully suffered, but we never get closer to delicious.

The puritanical beliefs that shaped American culture greatly influence this pleasureless path. Puritan colonizers who sought religious freedom established communities based on the belief that hard work was the way to gain God's approval and reward. Humans were considered sinful by nature, and only through rigorous discipline could they overcome their corruption and find God's favor. True rewards for one's labor were to be enjoyed in the afterlife because earthly pleasures were temptations from the devil. This belief that one must *earn* pleasure and relaxation by doing enough work colors the collective consciousness of American culture.

The tactic of depriving someone, or a group of people, of self-enjoyment and intrinsic worthiness is an intentional control mechanism. By depriving someone of an essential pleasure (peace, relaxation, a sense of worthiness, sensuality) and maintaining authority over that pleasure, you can control a person by doling out the reward for your own benefit. The beauty industry knows this. It robs us of our intrinsic worthiness, and tells us that we are born corrupt and in need of salvation. It tells us we must earn approval through products and procedures. It insists that carbs pose a dangerous temptation, and that we must deprive ourselves of satisfaction in order to look good in our clothing. "You must suffer to be beautiful," the mantra goes. *You must earn the worthiness of beauty through pain.*

This works, as long as women don't realize that "delicious" is our birthright. In fact, enjoying one's self and delighting in pleasure, without earning it, is essential to discovering our True Selves. If you like being yourself, and you know yourself as enough, then you neutralize anyone's power to shame and coerce you. If you're already living deliciously, then the devil has no power over you.

Would you like to live deliciously? is not, in fact, the devil's original offer but the very calling of your soul.

Years ago, I watched an inspirational video, the details of which escape me now. The part I clearly remember is when the speaker recounted a question his friend had asked him: "What if this is heaven?" Upon hearing that question, I paused the video and stared at the screen. The question struck such a chord in my soul that my ears were ringing and my mind felt tingly. "If this is heaven," I thought, "I am missing a once in a lifetime opportunity for much more pleasure."

A couple of days later, I walked into my local burger joint and glanced at the community bulletin board. A huge poster announced an upcoming author's talk on her new book, *What If This Is Heaven?* Again, my soul vibrated like a gong. So I started an experiment and decided to let that question inform, or at least influence, my choices. If I felt exhausted and in need of a nap, even if my to-do list towered above my head, I asked, "What if this is heaven?" And I took the nap. As it turned out, this pause made the rest of my workday smoother. If I was stressed out about being bloated and getting fearful around my food choices, I asked, "What if this is heaven?" In heaven, I reasoned, I would be happy enough not to care about bloating. So I lessened my worries. This began a positive cycle, where reducing my anxiety improved my digestion and bloating.

Each time I asked that question, I took back an ounce more of my power. Bite by bite, I was taking back the delicious life that beauty culture had held before me like a carrot at the end of the stick directing my life path. Now that I found myself worthy of pleasure and rest, I could ignore that carrot, and walk my own path to my True Self.

EXERCISE: What If This Is Heaven?

Perhaps you've tried affirmations before and found them ineffective. That's likely because your affirmations took the form of a statement, such as *I am healthy* or *I am confident*.

These statements can trigger automatic denial from the subconscious mind. We have so deeply internalized the opposite negative belief that the subconscious responds, "False!" just like Dwight Schrute in the TV show *The Office*.

Questions, on the other hand, invite the subconscious to entertain new possibilities. Instead of rejecting a new belief, your subconscious starts to notice evidence that the question may be true.

Use a dry erase marker to write "What if this is heaven?" on your bathroom mirror (as well as any other mirror you see frequently). Ask yourself this question during the day to gently nurture your True Self.

Self-Discipline

When was the last time you felt mama-bear energy? This is the fiery, powerful force that rises up when someone you love faces a threat. It says, "Nobody hurts my cubs!" You may have felt this if someone bullied your children, but this experience isn't reserved for biological mothers. My mama-bear energy activated when I came forward against my sexual abuser and I thought, "This man is not going to hurt another woman like this!" This protective energy holds tenderness and ferocity all at once, and is necessary to uncover your True Self.

The False Self develops to protect us from the various shapes of pain, including rejection, exclusion, harm, and discouragement.

Our subconscious mind won't let us live in the world without a sense of protection, so it holds on to the fortress of the False Self until we have another form of security in place. Self-discipline establishes the safe environment for our True Self to come forward.

Self-discipline is not self-deprivation. Deprivation makes us susceptible to manipulation, as discussed previously, whereas discipline fosters the environment and routines essential for uncovering our True Selves. Deprivation feels barren of compassion, and comes from the belief, "I am not worthy to enjoy my life." Discipline feels empowering and comes from the belief, "I am able to create an enjoyable life." Shawn Achor, an author on positive psychology, says happiness is the joy you feel moving toward your potential. If we use that definition, we find that discipline can be an experience of happiness, even if it's not one of immediate pleasure.

Freedom is an incremental process.

—WM. PAUL YOUNG

I healed my autoimmune disease because I implemented discipline around my eating habits. It wasn't easy at first. This new way of eating felt like a foreign language, and resources on grain-free diets weren't popular at the time. I stuck with my radical dietary protocol, however, because I saw it as a path to freedom rather than a restriction of pleasure. Even in the challenge, I felt the joy of moving toward my potential future without the threat of surgery and a lifetime of taking pharmaceutical drugs.

Every ancient spiritual path, which shares the goal of finding our True Selves, honors the importance of discipline. Consider the traditional practices of yoga, martial arts, or monastic lifestyles. Individuals underwent rigorous schedules of chants, meditations, and fasts. You could look at these ancient practices and say you see only deprivation.

Yet the individuals who choose, from free will and love, to follow these paths often do so because they experience the reward of their True Self.

Self-discipline also means removing yourself from toxic environments and influences that bully your True Self. Who are you letting bully your authenticity and your unique body? Is it the women's magazines that leave you with that inadequate and icky feeling about yourself? Is it the tabloid that shames other women's bodies and, therefore, your own? Are TV commercials telling you that aging is a hideous affliction? Are you hanging out with women who insist that dieting is the only way to achieve fundamental self-worth? You hold the responsibility to create protection and self-discipline around these influences that belittle your True Self, and you can do that through an "anti-harassment order."

EXERCISE: Anti-Harassment Order

Write out or type the following:

A restraining order is necessary to prevent further harm or damage to plaintiff, including her physical, psychological, and emotional wellbeing.

PERSON TO BE PROTECTED

[List your name, age, and date of birth.]

OBJECTS TO BE RESTRAINED

[Include any of the following:]

> *Specific TV channels or shows*

> *Specific social media accounts*

> *Infomercials for beauty and fitness products*

Tabloid magazines

Women's magazines that make you feel icky and inadequate

People who don't champion my True Self

In order that the objects to be restrained be prevented from further harassing behavior, they must not come into contact with the person to be protected in any way, including but not limited to: entering their home in print format or appearing on their phone or TV.

SIGNED BY [Sign your name]

Place this anti-harassment order somewhere visible. To your subconscious mind, this creates a degree of protection that encourages your True Self to come out.

Self-Forgiveness

Often, when I'm coaching a client, she'll tell me the cycle of her self-hate: "I know I should eat healthier, sleep more, and just treat my body better. But I don't, and I berate myself for it." She's shaming and blaming herself in an effort to treat her body better, but those ingredients can't solve a hate problem—only love can do that.

Such conversations continue along these lines.

"Has someone ever hurt you because they were hurting themselves?" I ask them.

Often, they'll tell me how one of their parents fell short of love because they were struggling themselves with addiction, workaholism, trauma, or codependency.

"Do you think they acted this way because they loved or hated themselves?"

They say some version of, "Because they hated themselves at some level. They were trying to numb their pain, and they didn't know their true worth."

Then I'll ask, "What impact did this have on you?"

They explain how it caused them pain, frustration, and perhaps spurred them into self-sabotaging behaviors to cope with a compromised home environment.

"Right. You were hurt by the shrapnel of someone else's battle with themselves. You were doing the best you could to survive. Do you think blaming and shaming them is ever going to help them stop this cycle of passing on their pain?"

"No," they'll say. Sometimes, they'll tell me that they have compassion for this caregiver who was in such pain, or are working to forgive them.

"What if you showed that same compassion and forgiveness to yourself? Do you think that would increase your chances of treating your body kindly?"

Real forgiveness has to let go of all expectations.
You can't expect a certain outcome, you can't expect
them to reply, you can't even expect to know who you're
going to be on the other side of it.

—SARAH MONTANA

We create False Selves to cope with a dominating, toxic environment. Then our False Selves inevitably inflict pain on others, including our bodies. "Hurt people hurt people," as the saying goes. While we hold responsibility for the pain we cause, we are not necessarily wholly to blame. Psychologist and researcher Philip

Zimbardo explains, "The majority of 'normal, average, intelligent' individuals can be led to engage in immoral, illegal, irrational, aggressive and self-destructive actions that are contrary to their values or personality—when manipulated situational conditions exert their power over individual dispositions." In other words, when our False Selves arise in response to a dominating environment, they do things our True Selves wouldn't imagine.

I often see women withhold self-forgiveness as a punishment for the choices they've made or how they've treated their bodies. Their underlying beliefs are often:

- "I caused so much pain that I don't deserve to love myself."

- "If I forgive myself, it excuses the ways I've treated myself/ others poorly."

- "If I forgive myself, I won't be motivated to become a better person. Holding on to self-hate ensures I will improve."

But the degree to which we withhold forgiveness from ourselves is the degree to which we can't love others.

For example, at puberty, I learned to see my body through my mother's eyes. She saw her body as flawed, so I saw mine as similarly damaged. When I unlaced my own invisible corset, however, my eyesight changed. I saw my own body as a soulmate, a wise being, a friend, and I realized her body was all that to me too! Hers was the body that gave me my *life*. Her body rocked me to sleep in the soft waves of her womb, and nourished me from the well of herself. Her body was not my curse but my ultimate blessing. It finally dawned on me—what the mystics say in various ways: others don't need to change to be worthy of love; it's up to you to change your sight and find them already worthy of love. Self-forgiveness clears the hate from our eyes, allowing us to see the world from our True Selves. As a result, we witness others in their whole and holy True Selves.

EXERCISE: Self-Forgiveness

Set a timer for seven minutes and start a letter to yourself: "I'm your False Self, and here's why you're a bad person."

When the timer rings, sign off on the letter as follows: "Distastefully yours, Your False Self."

Then set a timer for another seven minutes and write a letter that starts, "I'm your True Self, and here's why you are worthy of my unconditional love."

When the timer rings, sign off on the letter: "In everlasting compassion, Your True Self."

Read both letters. Then ask yourself: Which voice do I want in my head? Which voice will best assist me in living my potential, and help me have a loving impact on the world?

If you're like me, it's the letter from your True Self. Tape it to your bathroom mirror or place it somewhere where you'll read it each morning.

Our False Selves are a cultural phenomenon, installed in our psyches so we cultivate cultural values without questioning them. Ultimately, the False Self separates us from the love within us, and without us. How can we ever find body confidence and self-acceptance with that separation? We can't, of course. Which is why it's never too late to do the work of uncovering your True Self. It's not just for you; it's for every young girl who comes after you. She needs your self-love as much as you do. Show her how it's done.

Women, we have a job to do, and time is of the essence.

CHAPTER NINE

SELF-EXPRESSION

To honor the self is to be willing to think independently,
to live by our own mind, and to have the courage
of our own perceptions and judgements.

—NATHANIEL BRANDEN

One week after I moved from Seattle to Phoenix—where I knew only two friends—I was turning twenty-six and wanted to throw a small birthday gathering. One of my friends said, "You've got to meet Brenda, an amazing intuitive, I'll bring her to the gathering." The first thing I noticed about Brenda was how the air around her sparkled, as if she were trailing a cloud of fairy dust behind her. She wore bold glass jewelry, bejeweled jeans, and a similarly embellished leather jacket. Splashes of blue and purple tipped her short jet-black hair. Brenda is a woman who looks so much like herself that it makes her radiant and magnetic.

After connecting with her at the gathering, I set up an appointment to meet with her as a client. During our first session, we dove into a discussion about self-expression. She said, "Lauren, do you know how often women come up to me and say, 'I love your blue hair. I wish

I could wear my hair that way.' But I know that what they are really saying is, 'I wish I was brave enough to express myself . . . on the inside *and* the outside.'"

Clothes, accessories, makeup, hairstyles, and beauty products are inherently neutral forces. We can use them to express or repress our True Selves. What allows one woman to self-express may be the thing that represses another woman—there are no rules to this thing! However, we can't know the difference between self-expression and self-repression unless we do the work to become body confident and get in touch with who we are. Then we can use accoutrements of beauty to celebrate rather than submerge our souls.

RECLAIMING OUR OPINIONS

"I get what you're doing," a commenter wrote on one of my Instagram posts, "but I think it's a very personal choice. I prefer wearing makeup and dying my hair. I prefer the way I look with these enhancements. They make me feel better." She was responding to my before-and-after social media photo—the before with full makeup and the barefaced after photo. Her comment garnered many likes from other women sharing these beliefs.

But our preferences of what looks better aren't often our true opinions; rather, they're the result of mere-exposure effect and what beauty culture has programmed our False Selves to prefer. We *should* do what makes us feel good, but we tend to confuse looking good with the sensation of feeling good in our own bodies. For example, I feel physically better going without eye makeup so I can rub my eyes, cry when I want, and spontaneously jump into a swimming pool without worrying about my mascara running. I feel mentally better spending money on longer vacations rather than beauty treatments. I feel emotionally better now that I'm comfortable with a makeup-free face, and I feel spiritually better because I no longer believe I need to fight the signs of aging to be worthy of love.

When we're wearing the invisible corset, we try to feel good not by making ourselves comfortable, but by trying to make others comfortable. In her TEDx Talk, "Body Image: Not Just About Your Body," body image activist Jessi Kneeland drives this point home:

> The two most important things girls can be called is pretty and nice, and you'll notice that neither of those two things have anything to do with the little girl herself. Being pretty is about being looked at, and being nice is about making people feel good. The highest praise that we can get as a little girl is that we have given somebody else a positive experience.

This made me think about what a friend told me: "My daughter got her first phone, and soon she started doing the selfie thing, posting pictures of herself. I told her to turn the lens around and look out at the world." Young girls are taught that their bodies are for looking at and being judged, so they learn to relate to their bodies by looking at them, as if through an observer's eyes, instead of actually *living in* their bodies. How they appear to other people matters more than how the world appears to them.

FEMININITY

Historically, the oppression of women masqueraded behind cultural concepts of decency and femininity. In the Victorian era, it was "indecent" for women to masturbate or otherwise express sexual desire. In the 1950s, it was "indecent" for women to venture into the workforce because they were letting their families down and rejecting their femininity. This pattern remains in place today, with a sneaky change of wording. *Indecent* and *unfeminine* have been replaced with the words *ugly*, *fat*, and *aged*. Women receive these criticisms when our bodies are not profitable to the diet, fitness, beauty, and cosmetic surgery industries.

Consider, for example, that it's illegal for a woman to go topless in most cities. Women are often harassed or demeaned for breastfeeding in public or foregoing wearing a bra. Yet videos of topless women are found on every porn site, and breasts are sexualized to sell products in every industry. In our culture, breasts are unacceptable unless they're profitable. Further, media outlets, such as entertainment channels and tabloids, shame women for existing in bodies that are not generating sufficient profits for the beauty industry. These types of media call out celebrities for having cellulite, or body hair, or a belly, or wrinkles. Because these women's bodies aren't selling cosmetics, hair products, plastic surgery, protein shakes, or gym machines, they are *indecent*.

*When she stopped conforming
to the conventional picture of
femininity she finally began
to enjoy being a woman.*

—BETTY FRIEDAN

Culture represses women's True Selves through the gender role of femininity. This encompasses the expected behaviors, personality traits, and physical appearance a culture prescribes for the female sex. In past generations, the adjective *ladylike* was used to police a woman's adherence to the feminine gender role. "She's wearing a skirt that bares her ankles? How appalling!" "She's a suffragette? Voting is a man's role; she must be a perversion of the female sex!" "She's going to work and leaving her kids at daycare? She's rejected her motherly instincts!" Now it's, "She's letting her belly and face soften, she's going gray, and she's not wearing makeup? She's doing womanhood wrong!" At every point of women's liberation, our newfound freedom was criticized for sabotaging our femininity.

Feminine energy differs from the feminine gender role. In Chinese medicine, yin and yang describe opposing cosmic forces. Yin, or divine feminine energy, has a fluid, emotional, receptive quality, while yang, or divine masculine energy, is more assertive, driven, and grounded. Both energies are present in nature and in each individual to varying degrees, no matter man or woman. Some people naturally have more feminine energy and feel balanced when they bring those qualities to the forefront of their career, sexuality, and aesthetics. Other individuals have more masculine energy and express their True Selves when they emphasize that energy in their lives. Others enjoy shifting emphasis between masculine and feminine energy. Rooted in patriarchal values of control and domination, gender roles force expectations on both men and women that diminish our authenticity and true power. Only when gender roles dissolve will women and men be free to express the energetic masculine/feminine balance of our True Selves.

After legislation established many aspects of female equality, from securing the vote to Title IX, society had to employ a new way to uphold patriarchal values. Beauty culture began to fulfill the role that legalized gender discrimination once played. Now, a woman is blamed for failing at her femininity if she's not beautiful, toned, or wrinkle-free. Of course, it's impossible for a woman's clothing choices, voting ability, career decisions, or appearance to make her less of a woman. We aren't 10 percent *less woman* if we're fat or have gray hair. We aren't 10 percent *more woman* if we get breast implants or hair extensions. The question here is whether or not we're *behaving* femininely, with our time and financial choices. The real goal of this gender role is not—and never has been—tradition, family values, or even beauty. The goal of the feminine gender role is *to keep women in our place while we pay out the nose.*

The invisible corset *is a part of* the glass ceiling. It's the reason why criticism of a female politician's clothing, hairstyle, age, sex appeal, weight, and likeability harms or halts her career, yet a seventy-year-old man achieves the presidency amid jokes about his small hands and orange-tinted skin. His appearance provides endless fuel for talk show hosts' monologues, but it doesn't disqualify him from being an acceptable man, the way a woman's appearance makes her unacceptable to roles completely unrelated to her appearance. The invisible corset handicaps women's confidence at age nine, and then it ensures we'll always be too much or too little for our position in academics, politics, leadership, and motherhood: too fat, too thin, too sexy, not sexy enough, too old, too young, too done-up, too she-let-herself-go.

If it seems like ditching makeup, letting your tummy go soft, or quitting Botox requires the kind of courage the suffragettes mustered to march in the streets, that's because it *is* the same kind of courage. We are fighting the same patriarchal system that seeks to prevent women from making decisions about our bodies, our governments, our economies, and our Mother Earth. It's just wearing a different disguise: lip injections and Brazilian waxes instead of whalebone corsets and petticoats.

My great-grandmother's generation decided they were entitled to voting rights. My grandmother's generation decided they were entitled to equal education opportunities. My mother's generation decided they were entitled to pursue a career instead of, or in addition to, creating families. And my generation will decide that we are entitled to exist in our bodies without shame about our appearance, obsession about our weight, or fear of our aging.

THE FOUR PILLARS OF SELF-EXPRESSION

Being a *real woman* has nothing to do with how much you like the color pink, how thin or curvy you are, if you prefer lingerie or going braless, or if you prefer to put your career or home life first. Instead, it is how true you are to *you*. That's where the magic is. Once women decide to express their True Selves, not only do they live deliciously, but the societal structures that seek to repress us and our daughters simply *can't*. Those forces only have a hold on our False Selves, and our True Selves neutralize their power.

There are four pillars to that kind of powerful self-expression: clarity, permission, boundaries, and outrageousness.

CLARITY

In her bestselling book *Reviving Ophelia*, Mary Pipher, a therapist to preteen and teen girls, discusses how girls lose a sense of self during adolescence. They're asking the question, "Who do I need to be for others to like me?" rather than, "Who do I want to be?" Dr. Pipher watches this pattern continue into adulthood and writes:

> *Even sadder are the women who are not struggling, who have forgotten that they have selves worth defending. They have repressed the pain of their adolescence, the betrayals of self in order to be pleasing. These women come to therapy with the goal of becoming even more pleasing to others. They come to lose weight, to save their marriages or to rescue their children. When I ask them about their own needs, they are confused by the question.*

For much of my life, I held the perspective that if I made someone else feel better, I'd feel better by extension. I believed the sole purpose of my intelligence, my body, and my life was to please others. Putting others constantly before myself made me angry, and I had to repress that anger in order to remain "sweet" and "likable." While my life accommodated other people's comfort, I was not living in service to love and truth. Our self-expression is the gift we have to share with others, and we have a responsibility to share that gift.

When we don't know what we want—which is the same as not knowing who we are—we can't be of greater service. Self-expression requires we ask the question that the feminine gender role forbids women from asking: "What do *I* want?" When we answer that question, instead of finding pleasure by pleasing other people, we discover the truth of pleasing ourselves. The first step is *clarity*: allowing your body to show you what you want. The following clarity exercise is a practice of feeling, rather than logically reasoning, who you are.

EXERCISE: Conversation with Your Future Self

This exercise is most effective after you've practiced the writing or visualization exercises in chapter 6. Those practices increase your self-trust, encouraging your inner wisdom to come through.

Set a timer for seven minutes. Close your eyes, and take ten deep breaths. With each breath, feel your muscles melt and relax, starting at your toes and bringing your attention up to the top of your head.

In your mind's eye, see a door. Notice its style and color and the type of doorknob. Open the door, and find yourself in a space where your future self enjoys spending her time. It might be your dream home, a place in nature, or a public space. Allow the space to be whatever it is—you get in touch with your intuition to the degree you trust your first impressions. Look around this place. What does it smell like? Are there sounds? What does it feel like?

Now, you hear someone behind you, calling your name. Turn around and see your future self. She greets you. Notice what she looks like, and what she is wearing.

You feel an open invitation to communicate with her. So you ask her, "What would you like to make clear to me right now?" Allow the answers to come through visually, with words, or with sensations.

Exist gently in the space with her. There is no urgency, for she is always here for you. When the timer rings, thank her for her wisdom. Find the door from which you entered and leave the space. Open your eyes when you are ready. You may wish to make notes or draw images after this meditation. (To listen to a guided recording of this meditation, visit InvisibleCorset.com/futureself.)

PERMISSION

Reiki is a form of energy work in which the practitioner acts as a conduit for spectrums of healing energy. During my first Reiki session with my practitioner, Nina, I entered a deep Zen state as she moved her hands across my body to move energy. At the end of the session, Nina shared with me what she had "seen," the intuitive images she glimpsed while working. As she described the imagery, I teared up. It was as if she had seen the best version of myself and was offering me pictures of my highest potential. After our next session, I was eager to hear what she had seen. She said, "You can do this too, Lauren." When I received permission from her to trust myself, it felt like the door to my intuition swung open.

Thou hast permission at all times to
say "no," to change thy mind,
and to express thy true feelings.

—CATHERINE CARDINAL

Self-trust is the foundation for accessing your body's wisdom, but we're often waiting for permission to trust ourselves. With Nina's permission, I allowed my intuition to come through visually. I made a daily practice of sitting in silent meditation, asking my body what she wanted to show me. At first, I felt perplexed and struggled to discern intuitive insight from my wandering mind. But I recognized this was a learning process, and I committed myself to the daily practice of self-trust. Now, I have this avenue of internal guidance to gain clarity and insight. For example, when I'm faced with a business choice, my first step is not to run a spreadsheet or consult with a business coach— although I do implement those forms of support. Instead, I first tune in to my body, through a visualization, and say, "Body, what do you have to say about this?"

One of my colleagues specializes in helping burned-out and over-achieving women practice self-care. She told me, "Often, the primary thing my clients need from me is my permission. They won't give themselves permission to rest. They need that permission from me." If we wait for someone else, such as a practitioner, authority figure, or our cultural/religious/academic environment, to grant us permission to express ourselves, we might be waiting forever. Here are three areas where we must grant ourselves permission to self-express.

Permission to Feel Uncomfortable

I took my first ballet class at age fourteen, when I stood a head taller than the ten-year-olds in the beginning class. A panicked voice inside my head squealed, "I feel so awkward and uncomfortable! I feel naked in this leotard, and I want to leave right now!" But then I put my hand on the barre, and the teacher turned on the piano music. My muscles seemed to turn into the melody itself, and every cell in my body breathed a sigh of relief, saying, "This, this, this. I've wanted this my whole life."

Ballet quickly became the primary avenue for my self-expression and creativity. I believe it saved my life because my desire to keep dancing gave me the motivation to heal my autoimmune disease through nutrition. But in order to allow myself this, I had to go through a period of discomfort so excruciating that it felt like the intensity of my embarrassment would melt the skin right off my bones. Self-expression requires that you put yourself in new environments, initiate new conversations, and present yourself in new ways. Give yourself the permission to be inexperienced, awkward, and stand out like a sore thumb. That's where it starts.

Permission to Be Where You Are Right Now

When we hate our bodies, we buy into the narrative that we can't accept ourselves right now, that there is too much wrong with us. We withhold permission to feel okay with ourselves until our skin clears up, or we lose weight, or we have a partner, or we get a different job, or we obtain a degree. But there is no wrong way to exist in your body. Once you give yourself permission to be as you are right now, you stop fighting yourself, and you can move forward in life.

I remember the weight lifting off my shoulders when I realized, "Wait a minute. Ever since I got acne when I was twelve, I believed I couldn't feel okay with my skin until it was magazine-cover clear. But I don't have to hold myself to that standard! The only thing holding me back from accepting my skin is an unrealistic standard." When I stopped holding myself to the expectations skincare companies had for my face, existing in my body felt easier and gentler.

Give yourself permission to accept what you believe is wrong with you: permission to have acne or a soft belly or stretch marks, permission to be anxious or depressed, permission to have an eating disorder, permission to have trauma. Give yourself permission to accept the reality of yourself. As scary as it sounds, that's where the healing begins. You'll reduce the bullying, shaming self-talk that exacerbates your emotional pain and often is the reason for unhealthy coping mechanisms and negative emotions in the first place.

Permission to Rest

We cannot listen to our bodies or fully access our intuition from a state of stress. As discussed in chapter 7, being in a relaxed, parasympathetic state increases communication between your brain and body. Rest is a primary ingredient in creating radical shifts in your life, while exhaustion facilitates stagnancy.

Often, we use exhaustion as an unconscious strategy to avoid the truth. The truth might be, "If I slow down, I'm going to realize how unhappy I am in this relationship, but I'm afraid to leave my partner." Or, "If I slow down, I'm going to have to change my career path because this is killing my soul, but I'm afraid of turning my life upside down." Giving ourselves permission to rest is the same as giving ourselves permission to feel our lives. This is uncomfortable when we've committed ourselves to living an illusion. But when we learn to speak the truth with our bodies and self-express, we realize that feeling our lives is the purpose of living our lives.

EXERCISE: Permission Slip

In this exercise, you'll create a large permission slip, granting specific areas of permission required for your self-expression. When I shared this exercise on Instagram, women shared their own take on it. One woman used beautiful stationary and calligraphy, while I used a Sharpie and Post-it poster board for my example. Use the paper and writing implement of your choice, and put at the top:

[Your Name] is hereby granted permission to:

Then list out specific ways you give yourself permission to listen to your body and self-express. Use the broad categories I just discussed (permission to feel uncomfortable, be where you are, and rest) and consider specific, actionable examples of what this would look like in your life.

For example, your list might look like:

[Your Name] is hereby granted:

Permission to Be Uncomfortable
- *take a beginner painting class*
- *try a bold new hair cut*
- *wear my favorite fancy shoes to the office*

Permission to Be Where I Am Right Now
- *throw out all the "skinny clothes" in my closet that make me feel bad because I don't fit into them*
- *stop buying anti-wrinkle creams*
- *stop trying every single acne treatment available*

Permission to Rest
- *take an afternoon nap*
- *start a stretching routine before bed*
- *listen to an audiobook and crochet for thirty minutes a day*
- *take two days off a week from working out*

When I made my first permission slip, I didn't consider my own permission enough to start expressing myself, particularly in significant ways. Recognizing this, I asked myself, "Who else will I support by expressing myself and trusting my body?" Then I wrote a line at the bottom of the permission slip that said,

Permission is granted by:

I wrote, "The women who will read my book." I also wrote, "My future partner," because I wanted to be the best person I could in this future relationship. I even granted myself permission from role models who came before me, such as Betty Friedan and Gloria Steinem, because—I imagined—they would want me to take advantage of their work and how they modeled self-expression and courage.

You might write:

my present/future children
my present/future clients or students
my role models

BOUNDARIES

When you can't say *no* to other people, you can't say *yes* to self-expression. We can only trust our bodies to the degree that we assert our body's wisdom over our people-pleasing programming. Contrary to what we often believe, prioritizing our needs over other people's demands upon our bodies and our time is how we are of greatest service. We can only love others to the degree we love ourselves and our own bodies. If, for example, you are a boss who routinely deprives yourself of sleep and runs on caffeine, then you will accept this behavior from your employees. You are not loving them because real love would be facilitating an environment in which physical wellbeing is prioritized. Similarly, if you allow toxic relationships in your life, then you become emotionally depleted and can't be lovingly present for your children or partner.

A boundary is clearly articulating the needs required for your self-expression and then behaving in a way that honors your needs. When other people do not respect your needs, you change your behavior and interaction with them. Boundaries are not selfish; they are in service to the highest and greatest good. In fact, the people with the strictest, clearest boundaries are the people who are effecting the most positive change in the world. In her TEDx Talk, Isabelle Mercier-Turcotte said, "What you tolerate you worry about." Boundary setting means you tolerate less and, therefore, worry about less.

While surfing Pinterest, I found an unattributed photo on a page with the heading, "What Do Boundaries Feel Like?" The photo provided the best concise explanation of boundary setting I've read:

- It is not my job to fix others.

- It is okay if others get angry.

- It is okay to say no.

- It is not my job to take responsibility for others.

- I don't have to anticipate the needs of others.

- It is my job to make me happy.

- Nobody has to agree with me.

- I have a right to my own feelings.

- I am enough.

We often hesitate to set boundaries because we're afraid of another person's emotional response. We don't want them to be angry at us, or disappointed, or misperceive our intentions. Underlying our hesitation is the question, "Will you still like me if I make this boundary?" By setting boundaries, however, you are going to like yourself more. The responsibility for liking yourself belongs to you, not other people. As you become a good boundary setter, you will inevitably find yourself in relationships where you are respected and understood.

We're also afraid of other people making us feel guilty for setting boundaries with them. But, as Henry Cloud and John Townsend explain in their book *Boundaries*, if other people's emotional manipulation and guilt messages work on you, *that's your problem, not theirs*. We all have a choice in how we emotionally respond. We get to decide if we will be a pawn to others' emotional manipulation and thereby override our self-expression, our greatest gift to the world. The actions of loving and trusting our bodies are things to feel empowered about instead of being ridden with guilt.

Finally, we struggle to set boundaries when we believe we are obligated to manage how people perceive us. The internal dialogue goes like this: "If I set this boundary, someone might think I'm mean or selfish or careless. They are going to misunderstand my intentions. I'll need to explain myself to them." But you are under no obligation to make sense to anyone, and other people are not entitled to understand you. In fact, if you're making intuitive choices, many people won't understand you because intuition cannot be logically proved or analyzed. You've got to ask yourself what is more important: how your life feels to you, or how your life is perceived by other people.

EXERCISE: Saying No

Consider an area in your life where you are saying yes at the expense of your self-expression.

Maybe you always agree to take on the extra carpool shift. Maybe you make yourself available to be verbally abused by a family member. Maybe you haven't cut ties with your ex, even though you know the relationship is unhealthy. Maybe you want to have a morning routine, but you say yes to the vortex of social media upon waking.

When you have a private moment, imagine the situation or the person you need to say no to. Then say the word out loud, repeatedly. "No, no, no, no, no. Noppity nope nope. No way. Not happening. I'm done." I got this idea from a medical intuitive who told me I needed to simply practice saying no out loud. Laugh if you want—I did. But I tried it, and it helped. I found it profoundly cathartic, and would soon break into a chorus of "Noooooo" while driving in the car or taking a shower.

After this solitary practice, it's time to put your no into action. That action might be in an email, or a conversation, or a behavior change on your part.

OUTRAGEOUSNESS

In her bestselling book *Outrageous Acts and Everyday Rebellion*, Gloria Steinem explains how she often ended her lectures by making an agreement with the participants. If they would do one outrageous thing, no matter how small, the following day she would too. She wrote that this act could be as small as saying, "Pick it up yourself"—a brave boundary for women who have shouldered all the household responsibility. On a bigger scale, these acts could include requesting a raise, organizing a strike, or writing a feminist critique of a book and handing it out on a college campus.

Steinem reports two results arising from this agreement:

First, the world one day later won't be quite the same. Second, we will have such a good time that we will never again get up in the morning saying, "Will I do anything outrageous?" but only, "What outrageous act will I do today?"

To develop the habit of self-expression, I've found nothing as useful or effective than a little bit of outrageous, reckless abandon.

I do not believe that death should be allowed to find us seated comfortably in our tenured positions. . . . Instead, we should make use of our security, our seniority, to take risks, to make noise, to be courageous, to become unpopular.

—CAROLYN HEILBRUN

Powerful, meaningful self-expression catalyzes a chain reaction in our environment that we can neither predict nor control. We're letting some degree of truth loose, and it is the glorious nature of truth to touch everyone in its vicinity with electrifying sparks of life. Depending on your perspective of unpredictable situations, self-expression may cause you to feel either terrified or exhilarated. If you're anything like me, it's mostly terrifying.

The first time I made an online dating profile, I wrote forty-seven drafts of my bio before putting it up on the dating site. Then, for three weeks, I kept my profile on "Hidden." When I finally switched my settings to "Visible" and faced the option to swipe right on a profile, I paced my living room for twenty minutes, swiped right, and promptly suffered a heart attack. With sweaty fingers I deleted my account and collapsed on my couch as I tried to catch my breath.

This happened six months after a breakup, and my intuition had been telling me, "It's time to start dating again." Yet as soon as I got close enough to expressing myself and interacting with others on the dating site, the unknown outcome paralyzed me with fear. Finally, I realized I was procrastinating on my intuition. I was preventing unknown but important changes in my life because I needed to know what would come next. I wanted a plan. In fact, I wanted more than a plan—I wanted exact bullet points of what to expect from swiping on someone's profile so I could line up perfect responses and emotionally prepare myself.

I realized the best time to start—the only time to start—is when I'm not ready. So I equipped myself with the four magic words that open the doors to radiant self-expression: *oh, what the hell.*

"Oh, what the hell," I said before swiping left or right on a profile. "Ohwhatthehell," I muttered as I tapped out a message and hit send before my hesitation caught up. "Oh, good lord, what the hell!" I blurted out loud, as I agreed to a coffee date the following day. Gradually, the terror started to taste like exhilaration. This grand unknown didn't have to be scary. In fact, it could even be fun if I let it be.

Like love, trust is not just a feeling—it's an action. In order to express ourselves, we must trust our bodies' inner voice. Our intuition leads us forward one step at a time, and we don't get to see the path ahead. Trusting our bodies means, much to my dismay, that we don't get a bullet-pointed life plan. When we are living according to a precise plan, we're living someone else's life because our unique life path doesn't yet exist. Your body knows the way, but she's not going to give you a map. She can direct you only one step at a time, and she needs you to be a little bit outrageous and slightly reckless on the path to yourself.

EXERCISE: One Outrageous Act

Write down twenty-one outrageous acts to express yourself, and commit to doing one daily for the next twenty-one days. When you feel your hesitation rearing its head, say "Oh, what the hell," and do it when you don't feel ready.

Here are a few from my twenty-one outrageous acts list to spark your imagination:

- Get the short haircut I've wanted but have been too afraid to try.

- Toss all my underwire bras and replace them with comfortable, sporty bralettes, and vow to never again wear uncomfortable undergarments.

- Call my friend and set the boundary I've been avoiding.

- Post a certain photo on Instagram even though I'm afraid that some people won't understand or will take it the wrong way.

- Stop painting my fingernails and toenails because I hate the upkeep (and seal this commitment by tossing out my few bottles of nail polish).

- Drink prosecco by myself on Monday afternoon in my apartment building's hot tub.

- Make a three-course meal just for myself, complete with candlelight and roses.

- Wear my best outfit to go grocery shopping.

At a loss for other ideas? Consider that one of the most outrageous things you can do is make a decision based on what feels best rather than what looks best. Ask yourself where you're sacrificing your comfort or health in order to adhere to beauty culture's standards.

IT'S IRRELEVANT

In a *Vogue* video interview, drag performer Hungry shared a drag makeup and outfit process inspired by insect facial features and 1980s businesswoman attire. The result, which Hungry describes as "distorted drag," looks otherworldly, glittering, mesmerizing. The videographer follows Hungry stepping onto the Berlin subway, towering above other passengers, with a pink feathery headdress. People stare and someone snaps a photo. Then Hungry walks into a restaurant, sits down at a white-clothed table, and orders a schnitzel. Gracefully slipping off an insect-like prosthetic nose, Hungry sets it down on an empty plate, and takes a bite of dinner. Hungry says:

> *One of the first words I learned the meaning of in Berlin was just "irrelevance." A lot of the reactions I get are just not relevant to my life, they're just not relevant to who I am, to what I do, and to my story. I . . . just separate it from making an impact to people that I care about and then to not care about what the irrelevant people necessarily say or how they react.*

Hungry uses the tools of beauty culture for transformation: makeup, nails, hair, and heels. But rather than using these tools to self-repress, Hungry uses them for unrestrained self-expression, even at the expense of leaving others perplexed and astonished.

If you've never shown up as you on the outside before, the steps you take toward self-expression might make you feel like you're walking into a restaurant in 1980s bug-lady drag by stepping out of the house without makeup or donning the clothes you really want to wear. Take a cue from Hungry and remember that other people's judgments and opinions of your True Self are simply not relevant to your life. Sit down. Enjoy your dinner. And be well pleased with yourself.

CHAPTER TEN

LOVE

Beauty is life when life unveils her holy face.
But you are life and you are the veil.

—KAHLIL GIBRAN

We've been told we have to change our bodies in order to love them. That we have to lose weight, get clearer skin, get a face-lift, dye our hair. But changing someone before you can accept or merely tolerate them is the opposite of loving them. Love offers unconditional acceptance. Love says, "I will learn to see you for who you truly are. For you, I will override my societal brainwashing that convinced me you must disguise your True Self to be worthy of my love." Loving your body is not about making her look different, it's about looking at your body in a different way.

For years, I expected to feed my body junk food and stress but still be healthy. I expected to dance through injuries and still have muscle sprains heal. I expected medications to fix my disease without side effects. I expected my body to comply with my life plan, even though that plan wasn't in alignment with my body. But as I learned to truly see my body, I released her from those expectations that were out of touch with reality and didn't fit who she is. Love is not about forcing another person to change. It's about releasing the expectations we have forced upon that person and seeing that person as who they truly are.

It's not loving to perceive our bodies as a machine. No number of bubble baths, facial masks, affirmations, or other forms of "self-love fluff" will lead you to love your body if you are forcing false perceptions on her, particularly that she should adhere to the beauty standard. This is commercialized self-love: an easy way to go through the motions of love without actually doing the loving. It's the same kind of love a cheating partner shows you when he buys you flowers, apologizes, and says he won't do it again—for the third time. Self-love fluff is a cheap display of affection without the commitment to the action of love.

TRANSACTIONAL VS. TRANSFORMATIONAL LOVE

Our culture encourages us to have a pseudo-love toward our body called *transactional love*. This type of love follows the reasoning that if we take care of our bodies, they owe us, and will pay us back. It's the opposite of *transcendent love*, which seeks to nourish the life and soul of another being. Transactional love occurs in partnerships where one person gives in order to receive something. The reasoning goes like this: "If I clean the kitchen, or if I let them choose the movie, my partner will be indebted to me and will owe me some form of repayment (such as sex, dinner, a physical gift, and so forth)." This type of barter-based love is so predominant in relationships that we don't realize it is dysfunctional and controlling. Transcendent love is when you think, "If I do this action or get this gift, it will touch my partner's soul and bring them joy. I feel a sense of fulfillment in nurturing her this way."

In the same way, we practice transactional love when we expect repayment from our bodies. Consider how many fad diets and fitness regimens are marketed with the underlying message, "If you make better food and exercise choices, your body will repay you by being more energized, more productive, and hotter." Transcendent love, however, leads you to make choices because you want to nurture your body, just like you would want to nurture the wellbeing of someone you dearly love. The *means* of nurturing and loving is the *end*—there is no desired outcome because you are in the moment. Transactional love is motivated by fear because you're terrified that you won't be taken care of unless you use love in a manipulative manner. Transcendent love is motivated by trust because you know that if your partner, such as your body, is joyful and nourished, your relationship will flourish and lift you both higher.

WHAT DOES IT MEAN TO LOVE YOUR BODY?

Is it love when you silence your body instead of listening to her?

Is it love when you tell your body that you are ashamed of who she is?

Is it love when you verbally abuse your body by repeating that she is fat, ugly, and inadequate?

Is it love when you believe your body is not worthy of admiration until she is altered to look like someone else?

Is it love when you don't believe your body has the right to express herself through the signs of childbirth and aging?

Is it love when you compare your body to an illusory standard of appearance and behavior?

If we don't know what it means to love our bodies, it's because we don't know what it means to be loved. The way we've been treated determines the way we treat our bodies. Consider the ways you were silenced instead of listened to. When you were a young child, did you try to express yourself to your parents, only to be shut down? Were they too busy to listen to what you wanted or too self-absorbed to care about the art you had created? Were you ever told by your caretakers, teachers, peers, or leaders that who you were was shameful? Were you told your interests were wrong or your creativity was wrong?

When we haven't experienced unconditional, life-nurturing love in our lives, we can't give that love to our bodies. In order to experience a loving partnership with our bodies, we must recognize the ways we've internalized the belief that we are unworthy of love. We must learn to give our bodies the love that no one else gave us. In that way, we open the doors to true love rushing into our lives.

A YEAR OF BODY PARTNERSHIP

Until I tried it myself, I laughed at the concept of falling in love with yourself first. It sounded like the Hallmark epithets that make me break out in hives. After extricating myself from an abusive relationship, I knew I needed to set a new standard before inviting a new partner into my life. I needed to start recognizing real love, so I could say yes to it, instead of saying yes to the illusion of love offered to me by my abuser. For a year, I committed to love the partner of my body in the way I wanted to be loved by someone else.

I considered everything I had longed for in a relationship. I wanted someone who prioritized our time together instead of making me secondary to their work. Someone who said only loving things about my body, instead of nitpicking her appearance. Someone who looked at her with unrestrained admiration. Someone who took pleasure in giving me sexual pleasure. Someone who respected my work and honored the boundaries I set around my creative time. Someone who felt proud to be in public with me rather than insecure about me. I wanted someone who championed my soul.

In that year-long experiment, I intentionally remained single so I could focus primarily on being a partner to my body rather than to someone else. I showed my body how much I loved her through my actions. I implemented work-at-home office hours and respected this new boundary in my work. I booked solo weekend trips every couple of months. I made my body lovely dinners, complete with table setting and cloth napkins, because she was enough to deserve a date night.

I also began prioritizing my dressing and grooming habits differently. I made it my goal to appeal to myself rather than anyone else. "How do I make this purely enjoyable for me?" I asked myself as I scrutinized my morning routine. I stopped working at home in my pajamas, because my body was worth getting dressed for. I also donated all my uncomfortable clothing because, now that I was doing this for me, I wasn't going to make myself suffer.

Do not expect to receive the love from
someone else you do not give to yourself.

—BELL HOOKS

The "this is for me" mindset allowed me to relish the luxury I previously denied myself. I pulled out the silk bathrobe I was saving to wear for "someone special" because I didn't think I should waste it on "just myself," and wore it while I made myself breakfast. I began to dance naked in front of the bathroom mirror every morning, admiring my body's curves and her uninhibited movement. I started performing at poetry slams and published a book of poetry to show my support for her creativity. I started enjoying my time with my body so much that I began to tell her what I had longed for my whole life for someone to tell me: "You are magnificent, the way your soul shines out of you. I am grateful for every moment we spend together."

Most importantly, and for the first time, I was a relaxed woman. Can you imagine how it feels to slip off blister-causing heels, shed tight clothing, unhook your bra, and wash off your makeup, all at the same time? Taking off the invisible corset is like doing that to your *mind*. You'll have breathing room up there. When you're at home in your body, the world feels gentler and time feels kinder. Wearing a traditional corset makes relaxation physically impossible due to breath constriction and the artificially upright posture. The invisible corset is no different. As long as we wear those beliefs, we feel perpetually agitated and uptight.

A year later, I found myself in a completely new environment reflecting the radical shifts I had made. I was living in a new state, with new friendships, and a new lover. Our first night together, we stood in my kitchen hugging. We leaned our foreheads together, and I felt suddenly aware that his being extended beyond his physical body, like a shadow of light behind him. I immediately and unquestioningly recognized this as the tangible presence of his soul. Then, I felt something in this shadow click into place, like a tectonic shift, subtle but felt by every cell in my body. I silently asked the light. "What happened?"

"I just remembered," I felt the light say, "I'm supposed to care for you." The words entered through my body, inaudible yet distinct.

"And what am I supposed to do?" I wordlessly asked the light.

"You're supposed to be cared for," the light replied.

To be cared for. Tears stung my closed eyes as I realized, "This is what I've longed for my whole life: to receive love." In the last year, I had flung open the doors of my life to love, and it had flooded in. I didn't have to change myself, prove myself, or exhaust myself. I only had to care for my body in the way I wanted to be cared for. In that moment, I melted into my lover's arms and silently said to his soul, "Thank you, I accept."

As women, we've tried to make ourselves lovable by adhering to a destructive standard of existence. We've forced ourselves to silently endure physical, emotional, and psychic pain while smiling and looking pretty. We think this is the way that we're going to get the love we long for when, in fact, we're pushing love away. Your body has been waiting for you with open arms this whole time, saying, "I'm here to care for you." If you believe that your body makes you ugly and unworthy of love, you can't receive love from anyone else. When you see your body as who she truly is, however, you can finally receive the love the world has for you.

THE MOST SOPHISTICATED WOMAN

Every word and look and movement
spells Independence:
she likes being herself.

—EDWARD FIELD

In the 1954 movie *Sabrina*, Audrey Hepburn plays the title character, a young woman who learns how to enjoy life during a trip to Paris. Lovesick and without purpose, she leaves home to attend Le Cordon Bleu cooking school, following in her mother's footsteps. There, she meets an eccentric and elderly man who is infectiously in love with life. With the gentleman's help, Sabrina immerses herself in her new Parisian life, and she forgets her unrequited crush at home. Before returning home, she writes to her father, saying:

> *I have learned so many things, Father. Not just how to make vichys-*
> *soise or calf's head with sauce vinaigrette, but a much more important*
> *recipe. I have learned how to live . . . how to be in the world and of*
> *the world . . . and not just to stand aside and watch. And I will never,*
> *never again run away from life . . . or from love, either.*

She continues, "If you'd have any difficulty recognizing your daughter, I shall be the most sophisticated woman at the Glen Cove Station."

Indeed, she is unrecognizable, and it's not due to her appearance. Besides a haircut and new clothes, she resembles her old self. But she has been transformed by the dazzling shine that accompanies a woman absent of self-loathing. Sophistication and self-hatred cannot coexist because a sophisticated woman is in love with life, and therefore in love with herself.

Self-seduction means enjoying yourself for yourself. It involves attending to your body as you would a lover, tending to her with pleasure and admiration. When misused, seduction is behavior calculated to hide your True Self and manipulate another person. The most effective and rewarding form of seduction, however, entails enjoying yourself to such a degree you become magnetic. It's about arranging flowers on your coffee table, or dabbing on perfume before you sleep, or skinny dipping, or walking leisurely through the farmer's market with a basket on your arm and doing it for you. As a result, people look at you and think, "She's enjoying herself and her life so much, I want some of that enjoyment. I want to share that with her." Changing yourself to appeal to or accommodate another person is the opposite of seduction.

EXERCISE: Self-Seduction

Self-seduction means creating a life with your body that is so full of enjoyment that others want a taste of it. The practice of weekly dates with your body will build that life.

Plan a date with your body, as if she was a lover you want to seduce. This date could be a solo dinner out, a movie, a picnic, or a romantic bubble bath followed by your favorite self-pleasuring toys. Block off the time on your calendar, and prioritize it as you would a date with someone else.

Then write a letter to your body, inviting her to the date. First, mention a few instances when you enjoyed spending time with her. Make sure you speak in "we/us" pronouns. Start like this:

Dear Body,

Remember that time we [enter activity here]?

Examples:

> *Remember that time, four years ago, when we were walking in the woods and came into that sunny meadow, and we rested on the warm, soft grass?*

> *Remember that time, last Sunday morning, when we sipped coffee in bed and read before the kids woke up?*

Add a few more details to make this experience real to her again. Then invite her on the date you've planned.

> *I want to spend time together, just me and you. Here's what I have in mind.*

Some examples include:

> *Saturday night at the bookstore coffee shop, with a mug of chai tea and my cashmere sweater, because you love how that feels against your skin.*

Or:

> *Tuesday morning, let's wake up an hour early, and I'll make us breakfast to enjoy on the patio.*

Conclude the letter:

> *I'm looking forward to this time with you!*

> *[Sign your name]*

Then arrange the date with as much care as if you were doing this for someone else—because you are. If you're packing a picnic, put in the cloth napkins. If you're going out, enjoy the undergarments (or absence thereof) that make you feel most sensual. Seduction is not about the ends, it's about the means. If the process of preparing yourself for this date is not enjoyable, it is pointless.

After the date, jot a quick note to your body, just like you would text a lover after a date. Here's an example:

> *Dear Body,*
> *I had such a lovely evening together and can't wait to do it again. XO!*

YOU DON'T HAVE TO
LOVE WHAT YOU LOOK LIKE

The more I began to enjoy the experience of my body, the less I cared about her appearance. The body positivity movement told me I should find my cellulite, acne scars, thighs, and belly beautiful. But I didn't. That still felt impossible to me. So instead of trying to love what my body looked like, I started to not care and instead focused on positive experiences in my body.

For example, I love the feeling of sunshine on my skin, and I focus on that experience more than the appearance of my frequent acne breakouts. I love how my body feels in the hands of a lover, and I'm not detracting from my own pleasure by caring about how another person perceives my appearance. I love how it feels to hang out with my friends in the hot tub, and I don't care how my body "compares" to their bodies.

Author bell hooks writes:

> *Thinking of love as an action rather than a feeling is one way in which anyone using the word in this manner automatically assumes account-*
> *ability and responsibility. We are often taught we have no control over*

our "feelings." Yet most of us accept that we choose our actions, that intention and will inform what we do.

Instead of assuming that a warm and fuzzy feeling we call love determines how we treat other people, hooks encourages us to consider that actions first shape our feelings. If we take loving action toward someone, it can create loving feelings toward them. If we're waiting for a feeling of love to arise for our bodies, we might wait forever. Instead, consider *love* a verb. Are you living a life that shows love toward your body partner?

EXERCISE: Complimenting Beyond Appearance

Make a commitment, on social media and in personal interactions, to compliment a woman's contribution instead of her appearance. By doing so, you affirm that her worth is not her outer packaging or the investment she's made on beauty, but is deeper and more valuable. The more you train yourself to value other women's contributions as human beings rather than pretty objects, you'll increase how much you perceive your own value.

Here are some suggestions from eating disorder therapist Jennifer Rollin on how to recognize women's true worth:

You light up a room.

You have the best laugh.

You inspire me.

I love how passionate you are.

You make the world a better place by being in it.

You are one of the bravest people I know.

You make me comfortable to be myself.

You're an incredible friend.

You have a really refreshing perspective.

You are so smart.

You are truly making a difference.

Further, request that comments be about your contribution and not your appearance. If someone says, "You're looking thinner today!" you might say, "I appreciate your intention to compliment me, but I've spent too much of my life focusing on my weight. I'd rather be complimented on my insides rather than my outsides."

Here's what I say on social media when responding to both criticism and compliments of my body and appearance:

It's important to me that young girls and women look at the comments here and learn that they can be valued for the wisdom and ideas they offer rather than how much they conform to the beauty standard. To help me achieve that goal, please use the comment section to discuss ideas and experience rather than my appearance.

SELF-LOVE

In 2011, the World Health Organization reported that 40 percent of African women bleach their skin, using skin-lightening creams and products. In South Africa, Shingi Mtero teaches a course at Rhodes University on the politics of skin bleaching. She said, commenting on African women's desire for light skin, "Whiteness has been elevated and presented as a universal standard of progress. When people say it's about whiteness, it's not necessarily to physically be white, it's about wanting to access things white people have easy access to—privileges, economic and social status."

It may be obvious that black women who use skin-bleaching creams or Asians who undergo eyelid surgery are perpetuating racist values against themselves. But in the same way, when women of any race reach for anti-aging products, risky weight loss techniques, and body-modifying procedures because we don't feel good enough, we're perpetuating sexist values against ourselves. This isn't female empowerment, it's complicity. It's agreeing that our power is found by accepting patriarchal values instead of being entirely outside that value system. We're conforming to, instead of fighting, a system that grants men privileges that it withholds from women. This includes the privilege to exist without the shackles and expense of the invisible corset.

Jameela Jamil, a body image activist, uses the phrase "double agent for the patriarchy" to describe this phenomenon. Jamil explains:

The double agent for the patriarchy is . . . a woman who . . . is still benefitting off of, profiting off, and selling a patriarchal narrative to other women. [She's] selling us an ideal, a body shape, a problem with our wrinkles, a problem with aging, a problem with gravity, a problem with any kind of body fat. [She's] selling us self-consciousness. The same poison that made [her] clearly develop some sort of body dysmorphia or facial dysmorphia, [she is] now pouring back into the world. [She's], like, recycling hatred.

We are literally applying anti-women values onto, and into, our bodies. This isn't self-love; self-love is much more radical. Audre Lorde, a black lesbian poet and academic, published volumes of poetry and essays on the intersection of race and feminism beginning in the late 1960s. She famously wrote:

Survival is . . . learning how to take our differences and make them strengths. For the master's tools will never dismantle the master's house. *They may allow us temporarily to beat him at his own game,*

*but they will never enable us to bring about genuine change. And this
fact is only threatening to those women who still define the master's
house as their only source of support.*

Lorde was specifically referring to the strengths of women who
differed from white, middle- or upper-class feminists—those who
were poor, black, lesbian, and aged. That perspective is not only critical within the feminist movement, but it must inform our broader
goals as well. Women's strengths lie in our natural bodies—the very
aspects that make us different from the beauty standard. We can't
dismantle beauty culture by conforming to its anti-woman values.
Sure, we can find temporary power by wearing the invisible corset,
but it's never going to bring about genuine change, as Lorde points
out. Some women do believe that the invisible corset—the master's
house—is their only form of power. But how can a belief system
that fundamentally denies the innate wisdom and worthiness of a
woman's body give her true power?

Mary Wollstonecraft wrote what's considered the first feminist
manifesto, *A Vindication of the Rights of Women*, in 1791. She made this
same point, over 220 years ago. Wollstonecraft wrote:

> *Taught from their infancy that beauty is woman's sceptre, the mind
> shapes itself to the body, and roaming around in its gilt cage only
> seeks to adorn its prison [emphasis mine]. . . . Men have various
> employments and pursuits that engage their attention, and give a
> character to the opening mind; but women, confined to one pursuit
> and having their thoughts constantly directed to the most insignificant
> part of themselves, seldom extend their view beyond the triumph of
> the hour.*

By "triumph of the hour" she refers to the temporary power we
obtain through beauty preoccupation. While we feel a fleeting sense
of approval and desirability, we cheat ourselves out of the true power of
radical, love-fueled cultural change.

I used to think love was self-sacrifice. I thought it meant asking my parents, teachers, peers, friends, lovers, and the fabled male gaze: "What do you want from me? Who do you want me to be so that you feel good?" Hidden beneath these questions, of course, was the plea, "Please love me." Then, with courage and guilt and fear all churning in my stomach, I started to ask those questions of myself: "What do *I* want from me? Who do I want me to be so that I feel comfortable?" I realized I had misdirected my questions all along. I had only ever been imploring myself, "Please love me." That is self-love: listening to and honoring that plea within you.

The invisible corset cuts you off from your True Self, your power, and your joy. Self-love is unbinding yourself. Other-love is also unbinding yourself, because the *world* needs your True Self, your power, and your joy. Your children need it, your students need it, your friends, clients, peers, colleagues, and relatives need it. Mother Earth needs it.

We can only love others to the degree we love our bodies. One of my yoga teachers says, "If you can't see God in everyone, you can't see God in anyone." A woman who recognizes the worth of her own body will see the worth of every woman's body. When Beauty breaks the curse, she transforms not only the Beast but also the servants and her sisters trapped by the curse. We hold the same power as Beauty to transform—or rather, restore—all women into radiant, powerful beings. We only have to look at our bodies through the eyes of truth.

In his TED Talk, author and *New York Times* columnist David Brooks shares one of the toxic beliefs our society has bought into. He calls it the "lie of the meritocracy," and explains:

> *The message of the meritocracy is you are what you accomplish. The myth of the meritocracy is you can earn dignity by attaching yourself to prestigious brands. The emotion of the meritocracy is conditional love, you can "earn" your way to love. The anthropology of the meritocracy is you're not a soul to be purified, you're a set of skills to be maximized. And the evil of the meritocracy is that people who've achieved a little more than others are actually worth a little more than others.*

Our culture also bought into the lies of beauty culture:

- The message of beauty culture is you are your appearance.

- The myth of beauty culture is you can earn status by attaching yourself to beautiful people.

- The emotion of beauty culture is you're loved conditionally based on your appearance.

- The anthropology of beauty culture is your body isn't a wise being with whom you're in a partnership, it's a survival machine that you own.

- The evil of beauty culture is women who are more beautiful are worth a little more than other women.

These lies, sewn into the invisible corset, tie us so tightly we can't fully love. Men can't fully love women if we're beautiful objects that increase men's social status because love exists between *beings*, not things. Women can't fully love other women in friendship, workplace, and romantic relationships if we see each other's bodies as competition. Mothers can't fully love daughters if we show them how to wear the corset. Women of color can't fully love their ancestry when they see their bodies as a diversion from a white, European standard.

The opposite of every corset string—fear, domination, disconnection, mechanization, and coercion—is love. And love creates freedom.

A world without the invisible corset gives women the freedom to be who we're meant to be and to live lives that delight us, no matter what we look like. It offers the opportunity to be a woman without your appearance disqualifying you from a job, political office, leadership position, or a relationship. It allows women the freedom to have the mental space and financial capital to change our world instead of our bodies. It opens the doors for women to express their True Selves instead of shrinking their souls to be approved of by those who still insist that the corset defines womanhood. It's a world where women are entitled to body diversity and, therefore, body equality.

Of all the lies women tell ourselves, "I hate my body" may be the most lethal and the most untrue. We do not hate our bodies—our culture hates our bodies. Societal structures built on ownership and control hate our bodies. Industries that profit from women's insecurity and self-ignorance hate our bodies. Your body was never disfigured into the Beast. The only thing that was cursed was your eyes. They were covered up with lies so you couldn't see the truth and beauty of yourself. It's time for a great unlacing of the perceptions that make our bodies the walls of prison instead of the gates to freedom.

EPILOGUE

*Surrender means giving up the fight
between you and God.*

—CAROLINE MYSS

A few years ago, I booked a half day of Ayurvedic therapies. The treatments consisted of massage, an herbal steam, chakra balancing, and culminated in *shirodhara*, where a steady stream of warm oil is poured over the third-eye point between the eyebrows. As the oil began to flow onto my forehead, I felt as if a second pair of eyelids closed beneath my already closed eyes. I fell into a deep state, and I heard a question rising up from the absolute core of my being: "Who am I and where did I come from?"

That's when my soul showed me how it jumped into the earth. Imagine a six-year-old eager to take her turn on the high dive. She cannot contain the joy of herself, and she shimmers with phosphorescence. As I watched her approach the diving board, I did not know if she had jumped before, but I knew she could swim. The earth was the pool beneath, velvety black and threaded with stars. She jumps fearlessly, knowing she is everything she needs to be.

When you trust your body, you jump fearlessly into this beautiful world. You know you are everything you need to be to do what your soul came here to do. You navigate your life confidently and peacefully, even in the midst of crisis, because the compass of your heart guides your every step. You feel more deeply loved than ever before, because now you know the love your body has for you, and you love her back.

To trust your body is to surrender to her, to give yourself back to the one you belong to. We belong to our bodies, to the earth, and to each other—the whole human family is in this together. Now, more than ever, we need to give ourselves back to the wisdom we belong to, that wisdom within ourselves. It is the only guidance that will save us. When we've tied our bodies into the tight invisible corset of control, surrender feels frightening. The forces within us appear overwhelming—our appetite, our age, our intuition, our rage, our longing, our love. But what if we gave ourselves over to that ocean of untamed light? Author Elizabeth Gilbert says, "You're afraid of surrender because you don't want to lose control. But you never had control, all you had was anxiety."

Trusting your body allows for the fearless pursuit of who you truly are. Beauty culture prevents us from being true to our bodies, which means we cannot be true to ourselves. You deserve to experience a relationship with your body that makes you self-expressive and joyful. You are capable of following your intuition because your body asks nothing of you that you can't handle. You have the opportunity to be a loving partner to your body, and thereby attract loving partners into your own life. You can show your daughters, students, clients, and friends how to enjoy rather than despise their bodies. You can reject the anxiety of the invisible corset and finally be comfortable in your own skin.

Take off the invisible corset. Take a deep breath. And jump, fearlessly, into your life.

A LOVE LETTER
FROM YOUR BODY

My dearest companion,

This is to tell you what you often forget: I'm on your side. As long as our heart is beating, I'm here with you and for you.

I know we've shared dark times together. Perhaps you believed I turned against you, through disease or addiction or depression. I was not sabotaging you but speaking to you.

I know your greatest potential, the highest expression of who you are. Through hard times I was telling you, "You're not there yet! Don't stop here."

I teach you how to take care of yourself. You tell yourself you know best. You tell yourself you can eat all that processed food, or go on only six hours of sleep. So I must remind you: No, you can't. I love you so much I will not let you do that to yourself.

I am the voice of your soul, or at least its vocal cords. In times of turmoil, I help you discover who you are.

You may tell yourself that you can settle for an unhealthy relationship, continue the unfulfilling job, or withhold the forgiveness. Again, I raise my voice to say: "No, you can't." Because I love you, and I have your best interest at heart.

I loved you even when you didn't love me.

I remember the times you tried to hurt me, when you took a pry bar to my heart to excavate the pain. Perhaps it was an eating disorder or cutting or substances.

Even if you were letting the life out of me with a blade, or prevent-ing life's entrance by withholding nourishment, I was holding on to life for you. I was holding on until you gathered the courage to hold on for yourself.

Drowning pain with pain is so human and, therefore, so unshame-ful. I do not blame you for the self-harm. I never stopped loving you.

You listen to the voices of culture, the voices that chant inces-santly, "You are not enough, and you never will be." If you listen long enough, you will forget your mother tongue, the language I use to speak to you. The language through which I say, "You are enough—you always were."

More than anything, I want to speak to you. If only you knew the wisdom in this well of yourself!

The work of your life is learning how to listen to me. When you can hear me, you'll know you are always loved and you are never alone. You'll know that we can get through anything.

If you treat me like a machine, overworking and silencing me, I will burn out. But if you trust me and you ask me, "What do you need right now?" I will take care of you. I am more powerful than a machine, for I know how to heal myself.

I am not the machine but the mechanic herself.

Come home to me. If at first I seem foreign, it is only because you've been away for so long.

I will be with you the whole time as you remember how to be one with your heart.

I love you with every fiber of my being.

Love,
Your Body

ACKNOWLEDGMENTS

To those who supported, encouraged, and guided my writing: Heather, now I know what authors mean when they thank their agents for believing in them—thank you for believing in me! Nina, thank you for showing me what it looks like to trust myself. Brenda, thank you for your clear insight. Haven, thank you for your laser-sharp insight and for holding this book to its potential.

My gratitude also goes to those who blazed the trails that I now walk down: the activists for equality in all its forms. Thank you for your courage and conviction. Thank you for showing me how it's done.

I also hold deep gratitude to the women who've touched my life and taught me through their books, social media, and/or workshops: Mary Oliver, Elizabeth Gilbert, Martha Beck, Glennon Doyle, Oprah Winfrey, Anne Lamott. You have been my guides.

FLORAL SONG FLOWER ESSENCE THERAPY

To help my clients cast off their invisible corsets, one of the tools I use is Floral Song flower essences. These plant remedies shift trapped and repressed emotions in the body, facilitating heightened intuition, self-expression, and body trust.

During our intake session, I assess my client's greatest challenges in reconnecting to their body. This might include an inability to self-express, negative self-talk, shame about their sexuality, chronic anxiety, or repression of their intuition. Then I select flower essences that shift the emotional patterns related to that specific challenge. Using these tools, my clients see changes in as short as a month that can take years to achieve through mindset work alone.

HOW IT WORKS

Flower essences are plant infusions, free of allergens and without side effects. They shift emotions in the body—kind of like an acu-puncture needle in a bottle! Your body, like all physical reality, is 99 percent empty space, and only feels solid due to the vibration of atoms. Negative emotions carry vibrations that disrupt the healthy frequency of the human body. Flower essences work on a vibrational level to change these energy patterns.

Ancient cultures facilitated mindset shifts through plant medicines. They knew our perceptions hold us back from healing and wholeness. Modern science studies plants by grinding them up and analyzing the chemical components. This is like smashing a computer and trying to figure out how it works by studying the components. Plants work on an energetic level broader than chemical constituents. Floral Song flower essences capture the energy of a plant, offering a holistic therapy for mental and emotional shifts.

WHO CAN USE FLOWER ESSENCES?

Floral Song flower essences, which have no taste or flavor, can be dropped directly on the tongue or added to cold or room temperature beverages. These remedies help the whole family and can be given to children older than one year. When used as directed, flower essences are safe and supportive for pregnant and nursing moms. Many therapists, counselors, acupuncturists, and body workers integrate flower essence therapy to facilitate quicker, smoother personal growth for their clients.

WHAT TO EXPECT

When you use Floral Song, you'll notice unhealthy coping mechanisms and negative mindsets fading away. It feels easier to release stressful, anxious thoughts. The changes are gentle but monumental. Most people notice a shift within three days and more significant changes within three weeks.

You may notice some fatigue a few days after taking these flower essences, just like you might feel tired after an acupuncture session due to energy moving in your body. You might also experience heightened emotions for a day or so. This isn't a side effect, but rather an indication of the processing of repressed or trapped emotional energy.

HOW TO CHOOSE A FLOWER ESSENCE

Go to floralsong.com and select "How to Choose" from the menu for a quick quiz to determine your optimal flower essence.

BIBLIOGRAPHY

Epigraph

O'Donohue, John. *Anam Cara: A Book of Celtic Wisdom*. New York: HarperCollins, 1997.

Introduction

Brownmiller, Susan. *Against Our Will: Men, Women, and Rape*. New York: Open Road Media, 2013.

Orwell, George. *1984*. Boston: Houghton Mifflin Harcourt, 2017.

Chapter One: Beyond Body Positive

Cottom McMillan, Tressie. *Thick: And Other Essays*. New York: New Press, 2019.

Daly, Mary. *Gyn/Ecology: The Metaethics of Radical Feminism*. Boston: Beacon Press, 1990.

Denton, Elizabeth. "Here's How Much the Average American Woman Spends on Makeup in Her Life." *Allure*. May 26, 2017. allure.com /story/average-woman-spends-on-makeup.

"Eating Disorder Statistics." Eating Disorder Information and Statistics. Mirasol. Accessed November 25, 2019. mirasol.net/learning-center /eating-disorder-statistics.php.

Edraki, Farz. "Escape the Corset." ABC Radio National. December 19, 2019. abc.net.au/news/2019-12-20/south-korean-women-escape -the-corset/11611180.

Einstein, Albert, quoted in "'Do you live in a friendly universe?' Redux." Julia Colwell, PhD—Evolutionary Power. Accessed May 27, 2020. juliacolwell.com/archives/1926.

Etcoff, Nancy. *Survival of the Prettiest: The Science of Beauty*. New York: Random House, 1999.

Friedan, Betty. *The Feminine Mystique*. New York: W. W. Norton, 2013.

Gadsby, Hannah. *Nanette Netflix Special*. Directed by Maraleine Parry. Written by Hannah Gadsby. Distributed by Netflix. Release date 2018.

Gibson, Andrea. *Lord of the Butterflies*. Minneapolis: Button Poetry, 2018.

Gruver, Jackson. "Racial Wage Gap for Men." *Payscale*. May 7, 2019. payscale.com/data/racial-wage-gap-for-men.

Kuhn, Anthony. "South Korean Women 'Escape The Corset' And Reject Their Country's Beauty Ideals." NPR. May 6, 2019. npr.org/2019/05/06/703749983/south-korean-women -escape-the-corset-and-reject-their-countrys-beauty-ideals.

Leprince de Beaumont, Jeanne-Marie. *Beauty and the Beast: A Tale for the Entertainment of Juvenile Readers*. Urbana, IL: Project Gutenburg. gutenberg.org/files/7074/7074-h/7074-h.htm.

Lorde, Audre. *Sister Outsider*. Berkeley: Crossing Press, 1984.

McLintock, Kaitlyn. "The Average Cost of Beauty Maintenance Could Put You Through Harvard." *Byrdie*. June 26, 2017. byrdie.com /average-cost-of-beauty-maintenance.

O'Connor, Clare. "How Sara Blakely of Spanx Turned $5,000 into $1 Billion." *Forbes*. July 16, 2012. forbes.com/global/2012/0326 /billionaires-12-feature-united-states-spanx-sara-blakely-american -booty.html#269cb5687ea0.

Rhode, Deborah L. *The Beauty Bias: The Injustice of Appearance in Life and Law*. Oxford: Oxford University Press, 2011.

Saint Louis, Catherine. "Up the Ladder, Lipstick in Hand." *New York Times*. October 12, 2011. nytimes.com/2011/10/13/fashion/makeup -makes-women-appear-more-competent-study.html.

Shipman, Claire, Katty Kay, and Jillellyn Riley. "How Puberty Kills Girls' Confidence." *Atlantic*. September 21, 2018. theatlantic .com/family/archive/2018/09/puberty-girls-confidence/563804/.

"Terry Crews: The Resurrection of 'Brooklyn Nine-Nine' and
Redefining Masculinity." *The Daily Show with Trevor Noah*. Comedy
Central. Accessed May 16, 2018. cc.com/video-clips/9gugye/the
-daily-show-with-trevor-noah-terry-crews---the-resurrection-of
--brooklyn-nine-nine----redefining-masculinity---extended
-interview?xrs=synd_twitter_051718_tds_42.

Tolle, Eckhart. *A New Earth: Awakening to Your Life's Purpose*. New
York: Plume, 2005.

Townley, Chiara. "Cosmetic Surgery Is on the Rise, New Data Reveal."
Medical News Today. March 7, 2019. medicalnewstoday.com
/articles/324693.php#4.

Wolf, Naomi. *The Beauty Myth: How Images of Female Beauty Are Used
Against Women*. New York: HarperPerennial, 2002.

Chapter Two: Fear

The American College of Obstetricians and Gynecologists Committee
on Gynecologic Practice and the Practice Committee of the
American Society for Reproductive Medicine. "Female Age-Related
Fertility Decline." *Fertility and Sterility* 101, no. 3 (March 2014):
633–34. doi.org/10.1016/j.fertnstert.2013.12.032.

Bacon, Linda, and Lucy Aphramor. "Weight Science: Evaluating the
Evidence for a Paradigm Shift." *Nutrition Journal* 10, no. 9 (January
24, 2011). doi.org/10.1186/1475-2891-10-9.

Bauer, Katherine W., Michaela M. Bucchianeri, and Dianne Neumark-
Sztainer. "Mother-Reported Parental Weight Talk and Adolescent
Girls' Emotional Health, Weight Control Attempts, and Disordered
Eating Behaviors." *Journal of Eating Disorders* 1, no. 1 (December
27, 2013). doi.org/10.1186/2050-2974-1-45.

Brogan, Kelly, and Kristin Loberg. *A Mind of Your Own: The Truth
About Depression and How Women Can Heal Their Bodies to Reclaim
Their Lives*. New York: Harper Wave, 2016.

Columbia University Irving Medical Center. "Yo-Yo Dieting Linked to Heart Disease Risk in Women." March 7, 2019. cuimc.columbia .edu/news/yo-yo-dieting-linked-heart-disease-risk-women.

Dooner, Caroline (@thefuckitdiet). "Lots of people think they're addicted to food, but they are actually addicted to dieting." Instagram post. September 11, 2019. instagram.com/p/B2RyucpAB8d.

Enriquez, Erin, Glen E. Duncan, and Ellen A. Schur. "Age at Dieting Onset, Body Mass Index, and Dieting Practices. A Twin Study." *Appetite* 71 (December 2013): 301–6. doi.org/10.1016/j.appet .2013.09.001.

Fitzmaurice, Sarah. "Adele: 'I Would Only Lose Weight if It Affected My Health or My Sex Life.'" *Daily Mail*. November 9, 2012. daily-mail.co.uk/tvshowbiz/article-2229974/Adele-I-lose-weight -affected-health-sex-life.html.

Fortin, Jacey. "L'Oréal Drops Transgender Model Over Comments on Race." *New York Times*. September 2, 2017. nytimes.com/2017/09/02 /business/munroe-bergdorf-loreal-transgender.html?mcubz=1&_r=0.

Frankl, Viktor E. *Man's Search for Meaning*. Boston: Beacon Press, 2006.

Friedan, Betty. *The Feminine Mystique*. New York: W. W. Norton, 2013.

Gilbert, Elizabeth. Creativity Workshop. Hosted by Islandwood Special Events. Bainbridge Island, WA. April 1, 2017.

Golden, N. H., M. Schneider, and C. Wood. "Preventing Obesity and Eating Disorders in Adolescents." *Pediatrics* 138, no. 3 (2016). doi.org/10.1542/peds.2016-1649.

International Society of Aesthetic Plastic Surgery. "ISAPS International Survey on Aesthetic/Cosmetic Procedures Performed in 2017." Accessed May 2, 2020. isaps.org/wp-content/uploads/2019/03/ISAPS _2017_International_Study_Cosmetic_Procedures_NEW.pdf.

Kilbourne, Jean. "The Dangerous Ways Ads See Women." Filmed May 8, 2014. TEDx Talks video, 15:50. youtube.com/ watch?v=Uy8yLaoWybk.

Levy, Ariel. *Female Chauvinist Pigs: Women and the Rise of Raunch Culture*. New York: Free Press, 2006.

Lovato, Demi (@ddlovato). "This is my biggest fear. A photo of me in a bikini unedited." Instagram post. September 5, 2019. instagram.com/p/B2DLlZ4BfgP/.

Maines, Rachel P. *The Technology of Orgasm: "Hysteria," the Vibrator, and Women's Sexual Satisfaction*. Baltimore: Johns Hopkins University Press, 1999.

Mann, Traci, A. Janet Tomiyama, Erika Westling, Ann-Marie Lew, Barbra Samuels, and Jason Chatman. "Medicare's Search for Effective Obesity Treatments: Diets Are Not the Answer." *American Psychologist* 62, no. 3 (April 2007): 220–33. doi.org/10.1037/0003 -066x.62.3.220.

Miller, Kelsey. "Cellulite Isn't Real. This Is How It Was Invented." Refinery29. May 14, 2018. refinery29.com/en-us/what-is-cellulite -definition-fat-shaming-history.

Montani, J.-P., Y. Schutz, and A. G. Dulloo. "Dieting and Weight Cycling as Risk Factors for Cardiometabolic Diseases: Who Is Really at Risk?" *Obesity Reviews* 16 (January 22, 2015): 7–18. doi.org /10.1111/obr.12251.

NowThisHer (@nowthisher). "'Baby girl, you are beautiful. Black is beautiful.'—This woman gave an emotional pep talk to a 4-year-old girl who called herself ugly while getting her hair done." Instagram video. March 11, 2020. instagram.com/p/B9mkdo2FuBm/.

Okwodu, Janelle. "Thank God, Some of the Models at Couture Are Not Teenagers." *Vogue*. February 1, 2017. vogue.com/article /90s-models-couture-runways-age-in-fashion.

Oluo, Ijeoma. *So You Want to Talk about Race*. Reprinted. New York: Seal Press, 2019.

Porges, Stephen W. *The Polyvagal Theory: Neurophysiological Foundations of Emotions, Attachment, Communication, and Self-Regulation*. New York: W. W. Norton, 2011.

Rosenbaum, M., and R. L. Leibel. "Adaptive Thermogenesis in Humans." *International Journal of Obesity* 34, no. S1 (October 2010). doi.org/10.1038/ijo.2010.184.

Society for Nutrition Education and Behavior. "Health at Every Size." Powerpoint presentation. Haes Curriculum. Slide #30. Accessed May 2, 2020. haescurriculum.com.

Sweeney, Anna (@DieticianAnna). "Thinness isn't a cure." Instagram post. July 11, 2016. instagram.com/p/Bzxnfl9FM81.

Tribole, Evelyn, and Elyse Resch. *Intuitive Eating: A Revolutionary Program That Works.* New York: St. Martin's Griffin, 1995.

"The US Weight Loss and Diet Control Market." Research and Markets. February 2019. researchandmarkets.com/research/qm2gts/the_72_billion?w=4.

von Furstenberg, Diane. "Celebs' Quotes on Aging." E! Online. December 4, 2015. eonline.com/photos/17683/celebs-quotes-on-aging/537972.

Wolf, Naomi. *The Beauty Myth: How Images of Female Beauty Are Used Against Women.* New York: HarperPerennial, 2002.

Worland, Justin. "Why Loneliness May Be the Next Big Public-Health Issue." *Time.* March 18, 2015. time.com/3747784/loneliness-mortality/.

Chapter Three: Domination

American Society of Plastic Surgeons. "2018 Cosmetic Surgery Gender Distribution." 2018 Plastic Surgery Statistics Report. Accessed May 29, 2020. plasticsurgery.org/documents/News/Statistics/2018/cosmetic-procedures-women-2018.pdf.

Doyle, Glennon. *Love Warrior: A Memoir.* New York: Flatiron Books, 2017.

Eisler, Riane Tennenhaus. *The Chalice and the Blade: Our History, Our Future.* New York: HarperCollins, 1995.

Emerson, Ralph Waldo. *Self-Reliance.* New York: Charles E. Merrill, 1907. gutenberg.org/files/16643/16643-h/16643-h.htm.

Fraser, Laura. *Losing It: Fat Hopes and False Profits in the Diet Industry.* New York: Plume, 1998.

Global Hair Transplant System Market Report. "Hair Transplant Market Trends Research and Projections for 2018–2024." MarketWatch. February 25, 2019. marketwatch.com/press-release/hair-transplant -market-trends-research-and-projections-for-2018-2024-2019-02-25.

Hendrix, Harville, and Helen LaKelly Hunt. *Getting the Love You Want: A Guide for Couples.* New York: St. Martin's Press, 2019.

hooks, bell. *Black Looks: Race and Representation.* New York: Routledge, 2015.

Jim Crow Museum of Racist Memorabilia. "Anti-Black Imagery." Ferris State University. ferris.edu/HTMLS/news/jimcrow/antiblack/.

Kern, Stephen. *Anatomy and Destiny.* Indianapolis: Bobbs-Merrill, 1975.

Lattimore, Kayla. "When Black Hair Violates The Dress Code." NPR. July 17, 2017. npr.org/sections/ed/2017/07/17/534448313/when -black-hair-violates-the-dress-code.

Ledbetter, Cathy. "Men Are Getting Botox Now More Than Ever. These Plastic Surgeons Explain Why." Huffington Post. April 25, 2017. huffpost .com/entry/men-getting-more-botox_n_58ebf37de4b0c89f9120b2aa.

Lents, Nathan H. "The Relationship Between Waist-Hip Ratio and Fertility." *Psychology Today.* June 19, 2017. psychologytoday .com/us/blog/beastly-behavior/201706/the-relationship-between -waist-hip-ratio-and-fertility.

Lockman, Darcy. *All the Rage: Mothers, Fathers, and the Myth of Equal Partnership.* New York: Harper, 2019.

McClay, Cache. "Why Women Are Fighting Back Against Hair Oppression." BBC News. December 13, 2019. bbc.com/news /world-us-canada-50786370.

Mill, John Stuart. *The Subjection of Women.* Mineola, NY: Dover, 1997. earlymoderntexts.com/assets/pdfs/mill1869.pdf.

Moran, Caitlin. *How to Be a Woman.* New York: HarperCollins, 2012.

Ramsey, Meaghan. "Why Thinking You're Ugly Is Bad for You." September 2014. TED video, 11:54. ted.com/talks/meaghan _ramsey_why_thinking_you_re_ugly_is_bad_for_you?language=en.

Rees, Anuschka. *Beyond Beautiful: A Practical Guide to Being Happy, Confident, and You in a Looks-Obsessed World*. New York: Ten Speed Press, 2019.

Rhode, Deborah L. *The Beauty Bias: The Injustice of Appearance in Life and Law*. New York: Oxford University Press, 2010.

Santi, Christina. "Black News Anchor Fired After Wearing 'Unprofessional' Natural Hair." *Ebony*, January 16, 2019. ebony .com/culture/black-news-anchor-fired-unprofessional-natural-hair/.

Schucman, Helen. *A Course in Miracles: Combined Volume*. Mill Valley, CA: Foundation for Inner Peace, 2007.

Shahbandeh, M. "Retail Sales of Beauty and Personal Care Products in the United States from 2016 to 2019." Statista. January 7, 2020. statista.com/statistics/997359/us-sales-of-beauty-personal-care -products/.

Sjöö, Monica, and Barbara Mor. *The Great Cosmic Mother: Rediscovering the Religion of the Earth*. 2nd ed. San Francisco: HarperOne, 2012.

Solnit, Rebecca. *Men Explain Things To Me*. Chicago: Haymarket Books, 2014.

Wollstonecraft, Mary. *A Vindication of the Rights of Woman*. Mineola, NY: Dover, 1996.

Young, William. P. *The Shack*. Los Angeles: Windblown Books, 2007.

Zajonc, Robert B. "Mere Exposure: A Gateway to the Subliminal." *Current Directions in Psychological Science* 10, no. 6 (December 2001): 224–28. doi.org/10.1111/1467-8721.00154.

Chapter Four: Disconnection

Blake, William. "The Marriage of Heaven and Hell." 1793. bartleby .com/235/253.html.

Davis, Wade. "Dreams from Endangered Cultures." February 2003. TED video, 21:49. ted.com/talks/wade_davis_dreams_from _endangered_cultures?language=en.

Gilbert, Elizabeth (@elizabeth_gilbert_author). July 15, 2019. Instagram Post. instagram.com/p/Bz8s7GSBwe4/.

Kimmerer, Robin. *Braiding Sweetgrass: Indigenous Wisdom, Scientific Knowledge, and the Teachings of Plants*. Minneapolis: Milkweed Editions, 2013.

Lewis, C. S. *The Complete C. S. Lewis Signature Classics*. New York: HarperCollins, 2002.

O'Malley, Katie. "Kate Moss Regrets Mantra 'Nothing Tastes As Good As Skinny Feels' Nine Years Later." *Elle*. September 13, 2018. elle .com/uk/life-and-culture/culture/a23113786/kate-moss-regrets -mantra-nothing-tastes-as-good-as-skinny-feels.

Park, Yeonmi. "What I Learned about Freedom after Escaping North Korea." September 26, 2019. TED video, 5:10. youtube.com /watch?v=mLzTo-y8Ef0.

Porges, Stephen W. *The Polyvagal Theory: Neurophysiological Foundations of Emotions, Attachment, Communication, and Self-Regulation*. New York: W. W. Norton, 2011.

Price, Weston Andrew. *Nutrition and Physical Degeneration*. 8th ed. Lemon Grove, CA: Price-Pottenger Nutrition Foundation, 2009.

Schulz, Mona Lisa. *Awakening Intuition: Using Your Mind-Body Network for Insight and Healing*. New York: Three Rivers Press, 1999.

Taylor, Sonya Renee. *The Body Is Not an Apology: The Power of Radical Self-Love*. Oakland, CA: Berrett-Koehler Publishers, 2018.

Young, Jon, and Anna Breytenbach. "Tracking and Animal Communication." Nature Rocks. January 6, 2016. YouTube video, 10:51. youtube.com/watch?v=f-t5SaH8g3o.

Chapter Five: Machine

Beck, Martha. "Martha Beck on Burnout." October 30, 2016. YouTube video, 14:48. youtube.com/watch?v=jPjX2neOhS0&t=4s.

Chardin, Pierre Teilhard de. *The Divine Milieu*. 1st ed. New York: Harper Perennial Modern Classics, 2001.

Choi, Charles Q. "Peace of Mind: Near-Death Experiences Now Found to Have Scientific Explanations." *Scientific American*. September 12, 2011. scientificamerican.com/article/peace-of-mind-near-death/.

Drescher, Jack. "Out of DSM: Depathologizing Homosexuality." *Behavioral Sciences* 5, no. 4 (December 4, 2015): 565–75. doi .org/10.3390/bs5040565.

Dunn, Rob. "The Hidden Truths about Calories." *Scientific American* (blog). August 27, 2012. blogs.scientificamerican.com/guest-blog /the-hidden-truths-about-calories.

Entis, Laura. "The Case Against Counting Calories." *Fortune.* May 27, 2017. fortune.com/2017/05/27/calorie-counting-fitness-devices/.

Firestein, Stuart. *Ignorance: How It Drives Science.* Oxford: Oxford University Press, 2012.

Herschthal, Eric. "Frederick Douglass's Fight Against Scientific Racism." *New York Times.* February 22, 2018. nytimes.com/2018/02/22 /opinion/frederick-douglasss-scientific-racism.html.

Jensen, Derrick. *The Myth of Human Supremacy.* New York: Seven Stories Press, 2016.

Merchant, Carolyn. *The Death of Nature: Women, Ecology, and the Scientific Revolution.* Reprinted. San Francisco: HarperOne, 1990.

New World Encyclopedia. s.v "Entelechy." Accessed May 2, 2020. newworldencyclopedia.org/entry/Entelechy.

Office of Nutrition and Food Labeling. "Guidance for Industry: Guide for Developing and Using Data Bases for Nutrition Labeling." Food and Drug Administration. March 1998. fda.gov/regulatory-information /search-fda-guidance-documents/guidance-industry-guide-developing -and-using-data-bases-nutrition-labeling.

Park, Alice. "Scientists Have Discovered a New Organ in the Human Body. What is the Interstitium?" *Time.* March 27, 2018. time.com /5217273/human-body-organ-interstitium/.

Schiffman, Erich. *Yoga: The Spirit and Practice of Moving into Stillness.* New York: Pocket Books, 1996.

Sheldrake, Rupert. *Science Set Free: 10 New Paths to Discovery.* New York: Deepak Chopra Books, 2012.

Sjöö, Monica, and Barbara Mor. *The Great Cosmic Mother: Rediscovering the Religion of the Earth.* 2nd ed. San Francisco: HarperOne, 2012.

Spiegel, Alix. "Mind Over Milkshake: How Your Thoughts Fool Your Stomach." NPR. April 14, 2014. npr.org/sections/health-shots /2014/04/14/299179468/mind-over-milkshake-how-your-thoughts -fool-your-stomach.

Technical University of Denmark (DTU). "Gut Bacteria Affect Our Metabolism." ScienceDaily. November 21, 2016. sciencedaily.com /releases/2016/11/161121094111.htm.

Wheatley, Margaret J., and Myron Kellner-Rogers. *A Simpler Way*. San Francisco: Berrett-Koehler Publishers, 1999.

Wright, Jonathan V. *Why Stomach Acid Is Good for You: Natural Relief From Heartburn, Indigestion, Reflux, and GERD*. Lanham, MD: Rowman & Littlefield, Inc., 2001.

Chapter Six: Coercion

"(1981) Audre Lorde, 'The Uses of Anger: Women Responding to Racism'." BlackPast. August 12, 2012. blackpast.org/african -american-history/speeches-african-american-history/1981-audre -lorde-uses-anger-women-responding-racism/.

Biron, Bethany. "Beauty Has Blown Up to Be a $532 Billion Industry—and Analysts Say That These 4 Trends Will Make It Even Bigger." *Business Insider*. July 9, 2019. businessinsider.com /beauty-multibillion-industry-trends-future-2019-7.

Estés, Clarissa Pinkola. *Women Who Run with the Wolves: Myths and Stories of the Wild Woman Archetype*. Reprinted. New York: Ballantine Books, 1995.

Greer, Germaine. "Germaine Greer: Guilt Poisons Women." CNN. March 12, 2013. cnn.com/2013/03/12/opinion/greer-women-and -guilt/index.html.

McDermott, David. *Mind Control Manual: Vital Concepts about Mind Control, Cults, and Psychopaths*. Self-published, 2012. Kindle.

Mcleod, Saul. "Fundamental Attribution Error." Simply Psychology. October 31, 2018. simplypsychology.org/fundamental-attribution.html.

"Reese Witherspoon on the Abusive Relationship That Changed Her."
    SuperSoul Sunday. OWN. February 6, 2018. YouTube video, 3:43.
    youtube.com/watch?v=3CR7EeK-zUA.

Singer, Margaret Thaler. *Cults in Our Midst: The Continuing Fight
    Against Their Hidden Menace*. Revised and updated. San Francisco:
    Jossey-Bass, 2003.

Steinem, Gloria. *Outrageous Acts and Everyday Rebellions*. 3rd ed. New
    York: Picador, 2019.

Thomas, Shannon. *Healing from Hidden Abuse: A Journey Through the
    Stages of Recovery from Psychological Abuse*. Edited by Cassi Choi.
    MAST Publishing House, 2016.

Thurman, Howard. *The Luminous Darkness: A Personal Interpretation of
    the Anatomy of Segregation and the Ground of Hope*. 1st ed. Richmond,
    IN: Friends United Press, 2014.

Winfrey, Oprah. "Dr. Edith Eva Eger: The Choice." *Oprah's SuperSoul
    Conversations*. June 24, 2019. Podcast audio, 38:00. podcasts.apple
    .com/us/podcast/dr-edith-eva-eger-the-choice/id1264843400?i
    =1000442517079.

Chapter Seven: Listening

Beck, Martha Nibley. *The Martha Beck Collection. Essays for Creating Your
    Right Life*. Vol. 1. San Louis Obispo, CA: Martha Beck, 2013.

Buber, Martin Arnold. *I and Thou*. Translated by Walter Kaufmann.
    New York: Simon & Schuster, 1970.

DiAngelo, Robin J. *White Fragility: Why It's so Hard to Talk to White
    People about Racism*. Boston: Beacon Press, 2018.

Doyle, Glennon. *Love Warrior: A Memoir*. New York: Flatiron Books, 2017.

Eisenstein, Charles. *The Yoga of Eating: Transcending Diets and Dogma
    to Nourish the Natural Self*. Revised ed. Washington, DC:
    Newtrends, 2003.

Embrace. DVD. Directed by Taryn Brumfitt. El Segundo, CA: Gravitas
    Ventures. 2017.

Gottman, John, and Nan Silver. *The Seven Principles for Making Marriage Work: A Practical Guide from the Country's Foremost Relationship Expert.* Revised ed. New York: Harmony Books, 2015.

Hendricks, Gay, and Kathlyn Hendricks. *Conscious Loving: The Journey to Co-Commitment.* Reprinted. New York: Bantam Books, 1992.

Jeffers, Susan. *Feel the Fear . . . And Do It Anyway.* 20th anniversary ed. New York: Ballatine Books, 2006.

Moran, Caitlin. *How to Be a Woman.* New York: HarperCollins, 2012.

Peer, Marisa. "The Power of 'I Am Enough.'" Mindvalley. April 3, 2019. YouTube video, 3:06. youtube.com/watch?v=YYE0J-rMj-c.

Wheatley, Margaret J. *Finding Our Way: Leadership for an Uncertain Time.* San Francisco: Berrett-Koehler Publishers, 2007.

Chapter Eight: Discovering Your True Self

Adler, Alfred, and Colin Brett. *Social Interest: Adler's Key to the Meaning of Life.* Reprinted. Oxford: Oneworld, 2009.

Emerson, Ralph Waldo. *Self-Reliance.* New York: Charles E. Merrill, 1907. gutenberg.org/files/16643/16643-h/16643-h.htm.

Friedman, Zack. "Bestselling Author Shawn Achor on the Secrets to Happiness." *Forbes.* January 16, 2019. forbes.com/sites/zackfriedman/2019/01/16/bestselling-author-shawn-achor-on-the-secrets-to-happiness/#114110773e6e.

Greer, Germaine. *The Female Eunuch.* New York: HarperCollins, 2009. e-book.

Kang, Ning. "Puritanism and Its Impact upon American Values." *Review of European Studies* 1, no. 2. (December 2009). pdfs.semanticscholar.org/53e4/31bbbb8b33e3e713e6938c4bb02950ea22bb.pdf.

Kishimi, Ichiro, and Fumitake Koga. *Courage to Be Disliked: How to Free Yourself, Change Your Life, and Achieve Real Happiness.* New York: Atria Books, 2018.

Lamott, Anne. *Word by Word.* Read by Anne Lamott. Dripping Springs, TX: Writer's AudioShop, 1996.

The Lion King. DVD. Directed by Rogers Allers and Rob Minkoff. Burbank, CA: Walt Disney Pictures, 1994.

Lorde, Audre. *A Burst of Light and Other Essays.* New York: Ixia Press, 2017.

McDermott, David. *Mind Control Manual: Vital Concepts about Mind Control, Cults and Psychopaths.* Self-published, 2012. Kindle.

Merton, Thomas. *New Seeds of Contemplation.* Reprinted. New York: New Directions, 2007.

Montana, Sarah. "Why Forgiveness Is Worth It." March 2018. Tedx video, 15:53. ted.com/talks/sarah_montana_the_real_risk_of _forgiveness_and_why_it_s_worth_it?language=en.

Oluo, Ijeoma. *So You Want to Talk about Race.* Reprinted. New York: Seal Press, 2019.

Singer, Margaret Thaler. *Cults in Our Midst: The Continuing Fight Against Their Hidden Menace.* San Francisco: Jossey-Bass, 1995.

Thomas, M. E. *Confessions of a Sociopath: A Life Spent Hiding in Plain Sight.* 1st ed. New York: Crown Publishers, 2013.

Whitman, Walt. "Song of Myself." whitmanarchive.org/published /LG/1891/poems/27.

The Witch. DVD. Directed by Robert Eggers. New York: A24, 2016.

Young, Willliam. P. *The Shack.* Los Angeles: Windblown Books, 2007.

Zimbardo, Philip. "What Messages Are Behind Today's Cults?" APA Monitor. May 1997. Retrieved from csj.org/studyindex/studycult /study_zimbar.htm.

Chapter Nine: Self-Expression

Branden, Nathaniel. *Honoring the Self: Self-Esteem and Personal Transformation.* New York: Bantam, 1995.

Cardinal, Catherine. *The Ten Commandments of Self-Esteem.* Kansas City, MO: Andrews McMeel., 1998.

Friedan, Betty. *The Feminine Mystique.* New York: W. W. Norton, 2013.

Heilbrun, Carolyn G. *Writing a Woman's Life.* New York: W. W. Norton, 2008.

"Inside Hungry's Extreme Beauty Routine." *Vogue*. February 24, 2020.
    YouTube video, 10:25. youtube.com/watch?v=x4F_7SjE7Gc
    &feature=youtu.be.

Kneeland, Jessi. "Body Image: Not Just About Your Body." January 8,
    2017. TEDx Talks video, 16:34. youtube.com/watch?v=cWESkMN
    Pams&t=288s.

Mercier, Isabelle. "The Power of Zero Tolerance." June 14, 2016.
    TEDx Talks video, 20:05. youtube.com/watch?v=--mY5ruEhqI.

Steinem, Gloria. *Outrageous Acts and Everyday Rebellions*. 3rd ed. New
    York: Picador, 2019.

Williamson, Marianne. *A Woman's Worth*. New York: Ballantine
    Books, 1994.

Chapter Ten: Love

"Audre Lorde." Poetry Foundation. poetryfoundation.org/poets
    /audre-lorde.

Brooks, David. "The Lies Our Culture Tells Us about What Matters—
    and a Better Way to Live." April 2019. TED video, 14:46. ted.com
    /talks/david_brooks_the_lies_our_culture_tells_us_about_what
    _matters_and_a_better_way_to_live/transcript?language=en.

Field, Edward. "Mae West." Cultural Weekly. February 9, 2012.
    culturalweekly.com/mae-west/.

Gaskins, Tony A. (@TonyGaskins). "Love doesn't hurt you. Someone
    that doesn't know how to love hurts you. Don't confuse the two."
    Twitter. June 17, 2013, 10:29 p.m. twitter.com/tonygaskins/status
    /346816825755041792?lang=en.

Gibran, Kahlil. *The Prophet*. London: Wordsworth Editions, 1996.

Gilbert, Elizabeth (@elizabeth_gilbert_author). "Notes from the journal
    of a recovering control freak, shared with the greatest of love (as I
    gently loosen my white-knuckled grip on life . . . ♥)." Instagram
    post. February 24, 2020. instagram.com/p/B89qjCoBo7f/.

hooks, bell. *All About Love: New Visions*. New York: HarperCollins, 2001.

"Jameela Jamil on Banning Airbrushing, the Kardashians and Her Traumatic Teens." Channel 4 News. August 29, 2018. YouTube video, 48:05. youtube.com/watch?v=BXzO0z6fmhI.

Lorde, Audre. *Sister Outsider*. Berkeley, CA: Crossing Press, 1984.

Rao, Pavthra. "Paying a High Price for Skin Bleaching." Africa Renewal. July 2019. un.org/africarenewal/magazine/april-2019-july-2019/paying-high-price-skin-bleaching.

Rollin, Jennifer (@Jennifer_Rollin). "Non-Appearance Related Compliments." Instagram post. January 1, 2020. instagram.com/p/B6x0bsGFUst/.

Sabrina. DVD. Directed by Billy Wilder. Los Angeles: Paramount Pictures. 1954.

Wollstonecraft, Mary. *A Vindication of the Rights of Woman*. Mineola, NY: Dover, 1996.

Epilogue

Myss, Caroline. "Exploring our Irresistible Passion." Workshop. Hosted by Caroline Myss Educational Institute at Wedgewood Hotel, Vancouver, BC. November 5–8, 2018.

FURTHER RESOURCES

Books

Bacon, Linda, and Lucy Aphramor. *Body Respect: What Conventional Health Books Get Wrong, Leave Out, and Just Plain Fail to Understand About Weight.*

Eisenstein, Charles. *The Yoga of Eating: Transcending Diets and Dogma to Nourish the Natural Self.*

Friedan, Betty. *The Feminine Mystique.*

Jensen, Derrick. *The Myth of Human Supremacy.*

Levy, Ariel. *Female Chauvinist Pigs: Women and the Rise of Raunch Culture.*

Moran, Caitlin. *How to Be a Woman.*

Nagoski, Emily. *Come as You Are: The Surprising New Science That Will Transform Your Sex Life.*

Oluo, Ijeoma. *So You Want to Talk About Race.*

Sheldrake, Rupert. *Science Set Free: 10 Paths to New Discovery.*

Thomashauer, Regina. *Pussy: A Reclamation.*

Wolf, Naomi. *The Beauty Myth: How Images of Beauty Are Used Against Women.*

Group Coaching

My group coaching program, Food without Fear, is for those who struggle with eating problems, food challenges, and weight anxiety. After, you'll be able to trust yourself around food and eat intuitively, without weight worries. For more information, visit LaurenGeertsen .com/food-without-fear.

Instagram Accounts

Follow these Instagram accounts for support and encouragement in shedding the invisible corset as well as guidance for creating justice in the midst of beauty culture.

Ashlee Bennett, @bodyimage_therapist
Beauty Redefined, @beauty_redefined
Beyond Beautiful Book, @beyondbeautifulbook
Caroline Dooner, @thefuckitdiet
Dana Suchow, @danasuchow
Jennifer Rollin, @jennifer_rollin
Jes Baker, @themilitantbaker
Jessi Kneeland, @jessikneeland
Krista Murias, @kristamurias
Lauren Geertsen, @body_connection_coach
Maria Paredes, @with_this_body
More Love, @moreloveorg
Simone Mariposa, @simonemariposa
Taryn Brumfitt, @bodyimagemovement
The Body is Not an Apology, @thebodyisnotanapology
Virgie Tovar, @virgietovar

ABOUT THE AUTHOR

Lauren Geertsen is a Body Connection Coach who helps her clients overcome body anxiety and heal their relationship with food. She created the health website EmpoweredSustenance.com, now read by more than forty million people, and became a nutrition consultant after healing her autoimmune disease through alternative medicine. She's written one book of poetry, *Stronger than the Master: Poems of Manipulation and Escape*.

For information on her coaching, workshops, and speaking, go to LaurenGeertsen.com.

ABOUT SOUNDS TRUE

Sounds True is a multimedia publisher whose mission is to inspire and support personal transformation and spiritual awakening. Founded in 1985 and located in Boulder, Colorado, we work with many of the leading spiritual teachers, thinkers, healers, and visionary artists of our time. We strive with every title to preserve the essential "living wisdom" of the author or artist. It is our goal to create products that not only provide information to a reader or listener but also embody the quality of a wisdom transmission.

For those seeking genuine transformation, Sounds True is your trusted partner. At SoundsTrue.com you will find a wealth of free resources to support your journey, including exclusive weekly audio interviews, free downloads, interactive learning tools, and other special savings on all our titles.

To learn more, please visit SoundsTrue.com/freegifts or call us toll-free at 800.333.9185.